# From Cold War to *Ostpolitik*

*GERMANY AND THE NEW EUROPE*

# From Cold War to *Ostpolitik*

*GERMANY AND THE NEW EUROPE*

---

*by*

MICHAEL FREUND

*

TRANSLATED FROM THE GERMAN BY

R. W. LAST

OSWALD WOLFF

LONDON

First published in Germany in 1971
by Bertelsmann Verlag Gütersloh
under the title *25 Jahre Deutschland*

ISBN 0 85496 130 5



MADE AND PRINTED IN GREAT BRITAIN BY
THE GARDEN CITY PRESS LIMITED
LETCHWORTH, HERTFORDSHIRE
SG6 1JS

## CONTENTS

# TRANSLATOR'S NOTE

Michael Freund's account never strays too far from the relevant historical documents, and, where appropriate, official translations have been used, for example, in the case of the UN Charter extracts and the German treaty texts with Moscow and Warsaw.

I wish to thank M. S. Jones for reading the typescript and Dr. C. Baier for assisting me in checking the proofs.

R. W. Last

# CAPITULATION AND CHAOS

On 7 May 1945 three German generals, Feldmarschall Keitel, Generaloberst Jodl and Generaladmiral von Friedeburg put their signatures to the surrender of the German army in Rheims; and the signing was repeated in the Soviet headquarters in Karlshorst by Keitel, von Friedeburg and Generaloberst Stumpff. That, so it seemed, was the end. But it had really been all over long before, and it is something of a mystery that the Allies should have insisted on written confirmation of the collapse of a Reich which was already a thing of the past.

The full import of these documents cannot be judged by just looking at the surface of their text, which does not reveal the fact that at the moment of their signing, Germany ceased to exist.

The only explicitly mentioned authority in whose name the signatories of the capitulation were acting is the High Command of the German armed forces. The signing was actually authorised by the "Reich government" and the signatories were its agents. The Reich government is not named in the document, but it is absurd to claim that it was only the armed forces that surrendered. Total military capitulation can and does spell the extinction of a nation and bring about the political annihilation of its people. So the national government was surely deeply implicated. Not unnaturally, the victors demanded unconditional surrender, to enable them both to impose on the German people any terms they deemed appropriate and equally to ensure the utter subjection of the defeated régime. Complete military victory was to be the sole arbiter in future relationships with the conquered nation.

The objective of unconditional surrender on the part of the enemy was announced on 24 January 1943 by Roosevelt, President of the United States, at a conference between himself and Churchill, the British Prime Minister.

The reasons behind this step were clear enough. The decision had all but been taken to carry the war into Germany itself. Defeat was to be an utter holocaust clear for all to see. Hitler had sought to leave his people only the choice between total military victory and extermination. The demand for unconditional surrender was the Allied equivalent to Hitler's own refusal to recognise conditions in victory or even to contemplate a negotiated peace.

There were to be no peace terms in advance—in accordance with the terms of Wilson's fourteen points—on the basis of which the

Germans could challenge the peace. Besides, the victorious powers could never have agreed on a pattern for the new Germany.

This formula effectively excluded discussion on the content and conditions of the coming peace. A wall of silence surrounded the question of peace aims; only one objective was named : the destruction once and for all time of the power of the National Socialist Reich.

The Allies did not think beyond war with Hitler to peace with his former "subjects." They failed to recognise that National Socialism could not be defeated by force of arms alone, that the final and enduring defeat of Hitler could only be guaranteed by the establishment of a free Germany.

But what was to happen to the German people? Were they mere "potter's clay" to be completely refashioned, broken up and divided or left in one piece as a democratic or Bolshevist state?

Would the coalition of powers which had achieved victory over Germany retain their unity and govern Germany jointly, as had been their intention, or would it follow the pattern of previous great wars by breaking up as soon as the common enemy was brought to his knees?

For the British Prime Minister at least, the enemy was no longer Germany, but the Soviet Union. Once more he was toying with the idea which had preoccupied him in 1918; then too he had wanted to make common cause with the vanquished enemy, and put the Germans in the forefront of a crusade against the Soviet Union. In the years that followed, the struggle for Germany was strongly marked by the Churchill ideology, despite the fact that its other exponents were rarely as passionate, committed or brilliant in its defence as Churchill himself. He it was who asserted that Germany hung in the balance; and that the battle for Germany was now on in earnest. If the democratic powers did not take measures to halt the Bolshevist advance, he argued, then the USA and Britain would find that they had gone to war merely in order to substitute one kind of tyranny for another, by permitting the Soviet Union to succeed the Nazis as overlords of Europe. In all the great European capitals, in Berlin, Warsaw, Budapest, Prague and Vienna, the red flag was flying. Between the Soviet-occupied countries and the rest of Europe there rose an impenetrable wall; an iron curtain had descended, behind which there hung the silence of the graveyard. And it was not for that, thundered Churchill, that they had fought. Churchill strikes at the heart of a quarter of a century of German history : in the great pathos of his speech can be seen those aspirations which the Germans need not be ashamed to have felt. As Churchill repeatedly stressed, the Soviets must be thrown back to the frontiers of the Russian empire, the Poles, Czechs, Hungarians and Germans freed from the Soviet yoke and summoned to fight for their national independence. Like their forefathers in 1848, the Germans were exhorted to join battle under the banners of unity and liberty. The British and Americans, however, were sick of fighting. Now that peace had come at last and the main concern was for "milk for babies," the British voted out the man who had really won the Second World War, the man who spoke ceaselessly of fighting and greatness. The US army was disbanding itself, a process memorably described by Moritz Julius Bonn, former President of the Berlin Institute of Politics:

> Units of US Army troops were making their way back home on their own initiative. Things took place which in any army in the world should have been punished as mutiny; the railway system of the USA was all but choked with the floodtide of men demobilising more or less illegally. With an enormous effort, the USA had turned itself into a world power; now this position was slipping from its grasp because the "boys" wanted to go home to mum.

But the German people fought on—not with weapons of war, but drawing on their own inner resources—putting up a moral and spiritual resistance and constantly renewing their solemn pledge never to yield before the might of the Soviet colossus and never to recognise in their hearts a state which had come into being through criminal acts and injustice. They fought on like an advance guard which had no main army to back it up. But Churchill's assessment retained its validity, albeit in a watered down form, namely that the German question would one day be resolved as a result of an international power struggle. This did not take the form of a military conflict, although Kurt Schumacher continued to count on it. Fortunately peace was valued more highly by all concerned than the idea of "Germany," since after a great war nothing would be left of Germany and that would put an end to the German question once and for all. The struggle for Germany was a battle of words and proclamations, of thunderous diplomatic notes and rowdy but inconclusive international conferences.

The German people fought on for "freedom, justice and unity," for the right of free self-determination for their nation, and for the enduring human rights of freedom of speech and freedom of opinion. They were utterly convinced that their just cause would one day triumph over the vainglory of the tyrant.

The German people refrained from violence: the Federal Republic and all organisations, groups, and parties within its boundaries pledged themselves to pursuing their objectives by non-violent means. But, the opposition maintained, the ends which the

Federal Republic was pursuing were unattainable without violence. It came under severe attack because of its policy of non-recognition, as if it lay within its power to redraw the frontiers of eastern Europe and crush the GDR. The platonic protests and verbal non-recognitions—which had precious little practical effect—acquired an increasingly unreal and even nightmarish character, since there was no irresistible international power to back up their protestations. For all their impotence, these verbal and legal objections—which were overwhelmingly academic in nature—were regarded as serious threats, as an attempt to pave the way for a new world war which would seek to set aside the result of the one which had only just ended. The Russians maintained that German revisionism and revanchism—by which they meant attempts on the part of the Federal Republic to rectify some particularly glaring injustices on the European map—was but the long shadow cast by the war-mongering powers in the west.

But the battle for Germany had been broken off once and for all time in 1945; the shadows were all that remained.

Winston Churchill, years ahead of his time, called for an all-German government as the only way of filling the vacuum in central Europe. This was why he was even prepared to offer recognition to the tattered remnants of the Hitler régime, the Dönitz government, as the "government of the Reich." But the Americans concurred with the Yalta decisions: they did not want any kind of German government, and especially not one consisting of Hitler's former ministers.

On 23 May the Dönitz government was deposed, and also interned in a particularly shameful and unworthy manner.

On 5 June the new government of Germany presented itself to the Germans and the world at large in the form of the control council, a coalition government compounded of the four Supreme Commands of the armies of occupation, which announced in a decree that it was assuming the supreme governing power in Germany. Since the German armed forces on land, sea and in the air were utterly defeated and had unconditionally surrendered, and Germany, which bore the responsibility for the war, was no longer in any position to oppose the will of the victorious powers, Germany itself had surrendered unconditionally and Germany had submitted to all demands made upon it now and in the future. Germany no longer had a central government or administration capable of taking over the responsibility for the maintenance of order, the administration of the country and the execution of the decrees of the victorious powers. And so the control council became the strangest of all the "Reich governments" in German history. In its constitution it was stated that the Supreme Commander of the four powers held the ultimate authority in Germany, each in his own zone of occupation and "jointly in matters relating to Germany as a whole." In those few words, "matters relating to Germany as a whole," the fate of Germany was sealed.

But what is "Germany as a whole?" The following subordinate clause on the control commission's executive power was to prove the crucial deciding factor in the future development of German history: "whose decisions must be unanimous." In the control commission, just as in the United Nations, the tragic error of the veto was committed.

In the end it came to be accepted practice that the Supreme Commander acted on his own initiative in situations where no common agreement could be reached. This was the only possible outcome. It was hardly likely that the powers could be persuaded into agreement. But nor was there such a thing as a united Germany to challenge the will of even one of the victorious powers.

Now the zones of occupation were coming into being; and they were destined to determine the course of German history up until the present day, first to segment the country and ultimately to cause its final division into two separate states. They determined the future political order and structure of Germany. During the war the Allies kept on producing plans for the partition of Germany; but none of the joint Allied official war documents mentions the long-term division of Germany. The effectively completed division of Germany is the result of perfunctory efforts to carve the country up into artificial pieces. Germany was "simply" parcelled out into zones of occupation; but the dynamics of the occupation rule caused a divided Germany to come into being. The Supreme Commanders took up office as masters of their part of Germany in the spirit of a war objective: Germany was made "putty in their hands." The occupation powers infiltrated into German life, sought to transform it, to mould it after their own image. The division of Germany into occupation zones—as if by some jumped-up quartermaster—appeared to apply only for as long as the occupation lasted. But the boundaries of the occupation zones, worked out by a European council between July 1943 and September 1944 in the splendid surroundings of Lancaster House in London, now form the major lines of demarcation in Germany. No one in this council, apart from the Soviet representative, had a proper grasp of what this division of Germany really meant. So they drew thick pencil lines on a map of Germany, carving it up into three approximately equal parts; these were later to become the American, British and

Soviet zones of occupation. These crude and hamfisted cartographical exertions on the part of the delegation leaders were subsequently transformed into a precise treaty document by the experts; the boundaries of the occupation zones were neatly laid down in the text in due accordance with the legal practice of the Second Reich.

On the pencilled map in Lancaster House lay Berlin, which was to be occupied in sectors by the Allied armies, lost and alone in the middle of the Soviet sphere of influence. In the years of the control council "Germany" meant only what the USSR, the United Kingdom and the United States could be united about. And open and closed societies do not have a great deal in common. It was not exactly easy to construct a new Germany between the red devil and the deep blue western sea.

None the less common interests and involvement in the German zones ensured that in the early years a remarkably large number of the joint decrees of the control commission were actually put into effect. Many were born out of the necessity of the hour, many out of common hatred against the Hitler Reich—a sentiment which bound the Allies together even beyond the breaking up of the war coalition. Thus it was that the already embattled Allies could still agree on the decree proclaiming the dissolution of Prussia (25 February 1947). This resolution on the part of the control commission was little more than a gesture, for 1945 had already seen the smashing of Prussia once and for all time.

The occupation map of Germany had sealed the country's fate. The zones were the models upon which the new state and power structure in Germany was fashioned. The zonal boundaries assumed their definitive form when the USA resolved to stand by the Lancaster House agreement on the division of Germany into occupation zones; this meant withdrawal from the German territories held during the war which cut across the frontier between the Soviet and Western zones (especially Saxony and Thuringia). Surrendering Saxony and Thuringia went much further than America's previous restraint in not taking Berlin and Prague before the Soviet forces, which from a military standpoint would have been relatively straightforward, and by which it could have snatched the greatest prize of the war from the clutches of the Russians. This triple renunciation laid the foundations for the Soviet Union's unassailably strong position subsequently. But the USA, in contrast to Churchill, regarded the Russians as full allies and not as potential opponents in the new world struggle which emerged from the Second World War. So America let slip strong and decisive positions and advantages in the coming struggle for power in Germany. But the USA never gave up fighting for

Germany by all political and democratic means; it continued to pursue a German policy which could only have been successful through a violent and intense power struggle in real terms.

The USA allowed the Federal Republic to fight a battle for Germany which would only have been meaningful in the context of a broader international power struggle, a battle which the USA had lost way back in 1944 and 1945.

Without Saxony and Thuringia there would have been no GDR today; if they had not yielded up those territories, which are now central areas of the GDR, the American and British troops would not have reached Berlin and there would have been no West Berlin today. Whether such a situation would have brought the Germans nearer to a real Germany is not easy to judge.

The USA and Great Britain were resolved to press for the reinstitution of economic unity in Germany at the coming conference; they did not want the west to feed the cow whilst the east simply milked it. The USA went to Potsdam fully intending to have no truck with a divided Germany. A committee reported to the President that there was no likelihood that the zones of occupation would form effective boundaries for the internal division of Germany, and that they were wholly inappropriate as a basis for partition. The committee had to judge whether the old Germany could be parcelled out into meaningful natural units. That would only be practical, the committee declared, if it were possible to draw dividing lines in accordance with local geographical conditions. The two Germanies in their present form certainly could not claim to meet such standards. There was no need to talk Stalin out of dividing Germany. As far as he was concerned, Germany was whatever happened to be left of the country. And that could happily be left undivided. At the Potsdam conference this attitude formed the rock which the western Allies were unable to shift.

The question which arose again and again in Potsdam was: "What *is* Germany?" Stalin, however, did not tire of declaring that Germany in its 1937 frontiers could be used as a basis, excluding those territories which had been lost after 1945. The spokesmen of the western powers were stunned when Stalin told them what was left of Germany and how he succeeded in tearing piece after piece away from what did remain. Meanwhile the Soviet Union had placed German territory beyond the Oder-Neisse line under the "provisional administration" of Poland.

No secret was made of the fact that this would be more than just an "administration" and more than "provisional." The Oder-Neisse line had been established at the Yalta conference as the western frontier of Poland, subject to confirmation or renegotiation of the exact line of the frontier at the peace conference. The discretion of the peace conference—even had it been given any room for discretion—became invalidated by the far-reaching decision to make territories beyond the Oder-Neisse line into Polish territory, from which any Germans living there had to remove themselves.

And a population transfer such as this can never be a mere temporary measure. By presenting the Potsdam conference with a *fait accompli*, the Russians gave the Oder-Neisse line its terrible finality.

President Truman exclaimed to Stalin in Potsdam that the Allies had worked on the basis of Germany as it was in 1937 and had drawn up all their plans—for reparations, etc.—on this basis, but that Germany had now vanished overnight. Stalin countered with chill superiority that there was no longer a Germany in that particular part of the world. The Germans had all fled. It is all too easy to speak on paper about the 1937 frontiers. But where there were no longer any Germans, there was no Germany either. When Churchill drew attention to the fact that these areas had previously been the granaries of Germany, Stalin replied that someone had to do the ploughing and sowing. And the only people left there to do it were the Poles.

> Between the Oder and the Vistula, the Germans have deserted their fields, and these are now tilled by Poles. It is unlikely that the Poles would agree to a return on the part of the Germans.

The Poles—hiding behind the Russians' skirts—were resolved to "make a clean sweep" and to establish a purely Polish state. From the graves of the Second World War the ideology of the nation state rose up again triumphant, as if blood money enough had not already been paid to it.

The agreements at the Potsdam conference on the eastern frontiers of Germany and the population transfers marked a victory for the Russians and their cause. The city of Königsberg was handed over to the Soviet Union for all time and the Oder-Neisse line conditionally confirmed. The western powers received no more than verbal consolation.

The movement of population—either in the form of direct expulsion or flight—took its inevitable course. Western efforts to contain it were in Stalin's opinion not unlike bolting the stable door after the horse had gone. In these expulsions from the east almost one and a half million people perished.

The advance guard of the Poles who were to take possession of the country consisted—as has always been the case throughout recorded history—of adventurers, plunderers and even criminal elements who were seeking cover from the hangman in a land where they themselves could be judge and executioner. "Areas devoid of humanity, a no man's land empty of living creatures. bombed-out villages, destruction everywhere, a blistering heat," was how the landscape was described. Then the Poles put more constructive forces to work and turned these areas into inhabited, well-managed and productive regions.

For almost five hundred years the German national boundaries had remained unaltered. The great population movements of 1945–6 brought the first changes. And the closing of settlement areas after 1945 put an end to German colonisation in the east.

Bernhard Guttman has posed the question of whether, after the population transfer of the Germans in the east, the German nation still remained as it had been before.

> In nature regeneration of a seriously mutilated body occurs only in lower organisms; in higher forms of animal life the creature perishes if it loses a quarter or a third of its body volume. On the other hand, crystalline minerals are able to accommodate themselves to substantial reductions in size.
>
> The "spirit of the crystal" can cause the formation of a new and regular octahedron of reduced dimensions. It could be that the spirit of a nation, if it is still basically sound, could spontaneously reassume its former shape, even after terrible injuries had been inflicted upon it, by the subconscious operation of spiritual forces.

And in fact the horrible "amputation" did not deal a fatal blow to the German people.

It soon became evident that despite the horrific catastrophe the German nation had experienced, it still had not lost its vitality, and that although apparently already destroyed, it continued to live on against all probability—despite all the defeats and all the sacrifices; it turned in on itself, continued to resist destruction passively and silently, and therein lies the greatest miracle in the history of Germany since 1945.

## THE EAST-WEST STRUGGLE: GERMANY TESTED TO BREAKING POINT

Almost without exception, the decisions on Germany were forced upon the western Allies. They had to acquiesce, or else drive the Russians out of central Europe—if they had been capable of doing so. The only alternative was war. But instead of military conflict Potsdam initiated an insidious half-war, the so-called cold war, which in the years to come was to overshadow the question of Germany and its reunification. The President of the United States, Truman, lost faith in the idea that the future of Germany, Europe and the world at large could rest on a foundation of peaceful coexistence with the Russians. Truman wrote to his family that he had never seen such stubborn folk as the Russians. He did not ever want to have to sit down at the conference table with them again—but of course, he had to, despite himself.

The Potsdam formula for a solution of the German question consisted of a social and revolutionary reshaping of the country, of the "four D's" (demilitarisation, denazification, decentralisation, disindustrialisation), of an artificial ceiling on production potential and the establishment of a carefully planned subsistence level for the Germans.

But gradually the western approach gained the upper hand over such notions of world revolution. The victorious powers each carried out a programme after their own fashion and in accordance with their own social patterns: the Russians sponsored social revolution in their zone, the western Allies democracy in theirs, and rarely was there any common ground between them.

Such was the way in which a divided Germany came into being, and the originally military objective came to be realised of neutralising Germany as a real political factor, as a military and industrial great power, and indeed as any kind of influence upon the course of history. The Potsdam communiqué declared that the German people were now having to make amends for the terrible crimes committed under the leadership of those whom they had all too often applauded and blindly obeyed in their hour of success. The object of the agreement was to make open declaration of German criminality. German militarism and Nazism were to be stamped out, and the Allies would now and in the future unanimously take the necessary steps to ensure that Germany would never again threaten its neighbours or world peace.

It was not the intention of the Allies to extirpate or enslave the German people. It was the object of the Allies to give the German people an opportunity to prepare themselves for the future reconstruction of their lives on a democratic and peaceful basis. If they constantly directed their own endeavours towards this goal, they would be able to take their place among the free and peace-loving nations of the world in the fullness of time.

In accordance with the Yalta conclusions it was reasserted that there was to be no government of all Germany. The German question was to be dealt with in such a way that the political structure was to be decentralised and the development of local responsibility encouraged.

For the time being no centralised German government was to be established. However, this apart, there were to be created certain important central German administrative agencies.

The French objected to the establishment of such centralised administrative structures. Whether or not they would actually have come into being is an open question. The Russians were in favour for just as long as they could hope to exert the decisive influence upon a centralised German administration. In all probability it would have come to grief in the battle for control and domination. The west could not have tolerated a Bolshevist Germany, nor the Kremlin accepted a democratic one.

Western successes in Potsdam were largely verbal in nature. They demanded formal recognition of the fact that Germany should be a single economic unit. It is also laid down in the Potsdam agreement that reparations from the German people should not render it impossible for them to exist on their own resources.

Those were principles which would only be clothed with reality when the realities of life happened to accord with them.

De Gaulle, the head of the French government, also took the view that "Germany" was whatever remained of the country. He named the principal French demand after the war as "the permanent presence of French troops along the whole length of the Rhine and cutting off the left bank of the Rhine and the Ruhr from anything which in the future will form part of the German state or states."

No decision had yet been taken on these questions, but it was already becoming clear what direction future developments might be moving in. It was certain even at this stage that France would seek wide-ranging administrative powers and authority to rule in the Saar. But there was a world of difference between this and the population movements in the east. There were no expulsions and no one was driven out. The Germans stayed where they were. So it was already becoming evident that in the west of Germany no such violent upheavals would occur as had taken place in the east. The national frontiers in the west had remained unaltered for centuries and had not been subjected to redrawing like those in central and eastern Germany. As far as the German frontiers to the west were concerned, it soon seemed as if the Second World War had not taken place at all.

It was at this time that the USA completed work on the atom bomb. On 24 June President Truman informed Marshal Stalin of this world-shattering event that was also to leave an indelible mark on German history, which was to remain in the shadow of the bomb. For centuries Europe had been overrun by old-fashioned "conventional armies"—and this might still happen today. But from that time onwards, any power that attempted to strike across the iron curtain would risk the outbreak of atomic war, a conflict of nuclear bombs and rockets.

For a long time American policy in Germany had been based on the Morgenthau Plan—or, rather, on a diluted version of the Morgenthau Plan—as it had been presented at the meeting between President Roosevelt and the British Prime Minister Churchill in Quebec.

Morgenthau Jnr. had offered a very radical answer to the question of how Germany could be prevented once and for all time from ever becoming a military power again; namely, that Germany should cease to be an industrialised nation. It would be folly to rely on the "re-education" of the Germans, and to stop at military disarmament would only be solving half the problem. In an industrial age, Morgenthau argued, the industrial potential of a nation was also its military potential. So Germany's military potential should be destroyed by depriving the country of its industry. The arsenal of any rearmament, the Ruhr, should be completely demolished, the factories torn down and the mines flooded.

Of course President Roosevelt and Winston Churchill immediately denounced the Morgenthau Plan; the war ministry and the USA Foreign Office fought passionately against the objective of destroying Germany and letting the German people eke out a vegetable existence in a wretched historical and national limbo.

But all the plans which did the rounds of the American administration were really toned down versions of the Morgenthau Plan. German industry was to be cut down by roughly half, and the intention still was to put into effect a massive disindustrialisation of Germany.

The fundamental principles of the USA government for the military administration in Germany were in accordance with this policy. It was based on an "epidemic and civil disorder" formula. German industry should only be allowed to develop sufficiently to prevent the outbreak of epidemics and riots which could endanger the safety of American troops. In the famous document No. I.C. 1067, an instruction from the American government to Eisenhower, which for close on two years constituted the formal basis for the USA military government in Germany, the general was ordered "not to take any measures to reinstate the German economy or to maintain or advance German industry."

A Germany which was to have its industry "disarmed," should, in the view of the victorious powers, be in a position to hand over vast quantities of machines, production plant, blast furnaces, machine tools, and so forth. And so, the argument went, such a Germany would have surplus human resources if its economy were so radically cut back.

A country deprived of its industry would, if this view were accepted, need only a few machines and also only a fraction of its previous population. So the Russians demanded that armies of workers be recruited from the Germans and were determined to keep the German prisoners-of-war as workers. It seemed that the American Morgenthau Plan and the Russian demands for reparations were forming an unholy alliance.

There was only one snag: the lion's share of the booty was destined for the Soviet Union. It soon became evident, however, that the reparations were not only to be paid by the Germans, but by all of Europe, and not least by the western occupation authorities.

It was finally agreed that each occupation power should keep its own zone. In this way the character of the zones became more fixed, and the involvement of the occupation authorities in their zones intensified. On the other side of the coin, the discrepancies and imbalances among the zones also increased to a dangerous level. The eastern zone of Germany had to bear the whole burden of reparation under its masters. The Soviet Union, utterly exhausted by the war, really needed its zone and relentlessly milked it for years after the war.

Right up to the present day, the German question has been overshadowed by the steep "gradient" between one Germany and the other. The wall that divides them has served to protect the poorer Germany from losing its most vital forces to its richer neighbour.

Severe measures against free movement between the two Germanies have resulted in the effective creation of two "zones", the prosperous Federal Republic and the depressed GDR.

The Allies tried hard enough to establish a common subsistence level throughout the whole of Germany. A less disreputable version of the Morgenthau policy sought to reduce the German economy to a sleepy mediocrity, in which the only industries permitted would be agriculture and light industry, serving peaceful ends—a nineteenth-century idyll emerging from the most terrible destruction.

It was not likely that the two great world powers, the USA and the Soviet Union, would be happy to transform their respective Germanies into economic flower gardens.

But the shape of the economy and the level of industrial activity were not the only things to be imposed on the German people. They were also to be set—perhaps not permanently, but at least for the period of occupation—a specific standard of living which should not be allowed to rise above the average level for Europe excluding the United Kingdom and the USSR. This formula demonstrates, in the words of a great German economist, the ability of diplomats to "preserve the appearance of unity in the face of the most fundamental divergences of opinion; to pretend that problems which remain unsolved have none the less been solved; to cloak barbaric acts in fine smug phrases; and to present economic monstrosities in straightforward and seemingly lucid logical formulae."

Once more American evangelism and idealism in search of peace had come up against the realities of brute force. The USA had set out on a crusade whose aim was to rebuild Germany from the ground up. After the First World War the American ideals could still have operated in Germany's favour. But during the Second World War this Germany took on the appearance of the rottenest apple in the European basket, as the product of European lust for power, of racialism, of the darkest ages of the European past. In 1945 this American delusion led them to the view that it would be for the best if Germany in the future were reduced to a nonentity, because as a power and a state it knew no better than to become evil and dangerous.

Soon it became evident that it was more or less impossible to leave a void in the centre of Europe. It was very swiftly realised that any lack of order within Europe would inevitably turn into a centre of contagion. On the surface, the American military continued their devastation of German industry, while at the same time declaring that the famous order I.C. 1067 was utterly impractical. The Supreme Commander Allied Forces in Europe, General Eisenhower, the military governor of the American zone, wrote to the President that his staff and himself were of the opinion that production in the Ruhr must be started up again in the interest of the USA.

Without coal there would be an economic disaster. Without coal the transport industry could not be put back on its feet again, and without transport the entire economy of the country would inevitably remain crippled.

There was no point in a Morgenthau Plan unless it was carried through with the pitilessness of a Stalin or a Hitler prepared to let millions starve to death. After a time the morale of any army of occupation suffers if it has to live in the midst of poverty, filth, and degradation. The military authorities cheekily skated round order I.C. 1067. For indeed, everything they were doing sought to inhibit the outbreak of disease and disorder. No country can be ruled in the spirit of total submission, not even by military force. History has demonstrated that the moment of total military victory is rarely, if ever, a time for clearheaded thinking for the future.

The relationship between victor and vanquished, between omnipotence and impotence, such as exists immediately after the cessation of hostilities, can never form the basis of an enduring relationship between the nations concerned. In the years immediately following upon victory the seeds of a new positive growth can all too readily be trampled to dust. The memory of the days after victory and the folly of the Soviet Union's reparations policy has stood between the German people and the Soviet Union. The whole zone was searched for anything that could be dismantled and taken away. The ceaseless procession of goods trains gave the impression that a huge secondhand shop was being removed; and because it could not be taken, all the most valuable machinery had been reduced to rubble. It was a long time before the GDR recovered from the blood-letting of 1945–6. For many years the people of the GDR lived the dream of finding security in the refuge of a free Germany, but hopes of realising this dream grew fainter and fainter and the demands for liberation were watered down in the need for the most basic essentials. The fact that the Soviet occupation authorities re-established German political life more rapidly than the western powers did precious little in this direction. German administrative systems were instituted in the Soviet zone as early as 27 July 1945. Political parties were allowed to exist again; that is, the Communist party—appearing in innumerable disguises—was permitted to exist.

On 19 April 1946 the Communist party tried to become the majority party by the back door, by "annexing" the Social Democratic party, at least in Berlin. Those seeking to seize power tried to absorb the Social Democrats into the Communist dominated German Socialist Unity Party. The enterprise succeeded in eastern Germany.

In Berlin the battle of the parties was on in earnest. The influence of the Soviet Union and the Soviet zonal authorities reached into the city. A hard battle was fought for every local group of the Social Democrats. Kurt Schumacher and Herbert Wehner led the fight for independent democratic socialism in Berlin and at the same time for a free and independent Berlin. Their victory was of great historical moment. If the Social Democratic party, which was at its most lively in Berlin in 1946, had slipped into the clutches of the Communist party, then Berlin itself would have fallen into Soviet hands.

Even then this slogan was being aired: The unity of the working classes is the unity of Germany.

But none of the power groups succeeded in crossing the armistice lines of 1945. The empires of the two world political systems still have their boundaries in the same place as when the fighting stopped in 1945.

Each of the occupying powers penetrated more deeply into German life than had been envisaged in the Potsdam agreement. Two Germanies came into being, with different ways of life, different legal systems, and founded on different ideological principles. In the summer and autumn the first major incursion into the social fabric of the old Germany took place in the Soviet zone. On 10 September 1945 the land reform was announced which was directed towards those in the Soviet zone without land of their own. It was said that

> Through the land reform the centuries-old dream of the landless and low acreage peasants and countryworkers will be realised by the transfer of the large estates into their possession.

If this had gone no further than the law itself laid down, then this land reform would have been a unifying factor in Germany. For the nobility and landed classes east of the Elbe had survived the revolution of 1918, the Weimar Republic and the Third Reich. The land reform in the Soviet zone would finally have done away with this class which for centuries had ruled Prussia.

But no free peasant class came into being. The western zones of occupation—which soon became united in a single zone—came to have less and less in common with the eastern zone. The question was often raised as to whether Germany was divided because the GDR was Communist, or whether the GDR was Communist because the Allies intended to neutralise Germany and hold it in a state of suspended animation. The former Allies met again and again in order to prepare a peace settlement with Germany.

That the powers considered this to be a matter of urgency is demonstrated by the fact that they kept on meeting, although they knew only too well that their attitude and interests were irreconcilable. It is amazing to record how at every conference the powers blithely kept putting forward demands which they knew full well—

The British Foreign Minister, Bevin, stated that Britain would never again make the mistake that it did in 1918, that of taking away their old worn-out machinery and then giving them money to buy the newest and most modern equipment. But history was about to repeat itself. The Marshall Plan and the currency reform were just round the corner. German industry was again able to make a new start with the latest in modern machinery.

There is little wonder that individuals and nations alike would soon be saying of Germany that the Federal Republic by itself is quite strong enough.

One aspect of the programme of the supervision of Germany concerned the internationalisation of the Ruhr. The justification given was that such a mighty industrial power should not be left in the hands of a single state and especially not those of an unstable Germany. So an international administration for the Ruhr was set up in which the USA, Great Britain, France and Germany had three votes each, and Holland, Belgium and Luxemburg one vote. It was the task of this administration to undertake the apportioning of coal, coke and steel production in the Ruhr between German domestic use and export. Due account was to be taken of the vital needs of Germany. But these vital needs were to be decided by an international agency on which Germany only had three votes out of fifteen. When the Germans took their seats on this Ruhr committee, Konrad Adenauer spoke out, and his great opponent, Kurt Schumacher, castigated the Ruhr statute as a shameful instrument of oppression. If the letter of the agreement had been observed, the Ruhr would have come under foreign rule. In the commission Germany could be utterly voted down, let alone the men who had made the Ruhr into one of the greatest industrial centres in the world, who worked there, and to whom the Ruhr meant home and a means of livelihood. According to the statute, it was up to the commission to determine how much of the coal mined there could remain in Germany, and even in the Ruhr itself. On paper the Ruhr statute deprived Germany of sovereignty over the Ruhr. Adenauer knew that just as well as Schumacher, and still he was prepared to sign a treaty which even in his eyes was unjust and foolish. He relied on the fact that time would overcome rash judgement and unwise measures. And in fact all the treaty and European institutions which were still a hangover from the days of occupation have vanished like a bad dream. Adenauer was pursuing the classical wait and see policy which was founded on the hope that the spiritual strength of a nation will in the long run always win over the short-term power situation and the euphoria of victory, especially when they even run counter to the best interests of their own people. Schumacher did not want the SPD to become the party of a wait and see policy for a second time. It was his view that the defeat of the SPD when the Weimar Republic came to an end could be traced back to the accusation that its policy had represented an act of betrayal.

But policies of resistance or wait and see once again appeared problematical because of the experiences of the period following on the Second World War. In the Federal Republic the view gained currency that a nation could shave itself by yielding when the struggle appeared hopeless.

It was no accident that, in his efforts to obtain treaties in the east, Chancellor Willy Brandt acknowledged his indebtedness to the style and method of foreign policy adopted by Adenauer, although he had employed them in different circumstances, and to his resolve not to direct his foreign policy towards immediate advantage and quick results, but to allow things to develop and mature in the fullness of time.

Chaos in Germany could not be allowed to continue much longer. The economy was in ruins, and the German unit of currency—the Reichsmark—had become an empty farce, like the Reich which had given it its name.

The decision to set up a west German state was taken in June 1948 at a conference of the governments of the USA, France, England, Holland, Belgium and Luxemburg, which took place in London. By means of the Marshall Plan, which meant a gigantic injection of financial aid into Europe, America had brought into being European institutions and common agencies which administered the financial aid and which were later to bear fruit in a European economic community. A European economic community was unthinkable without Germany. For the sake of Europe some kind of Germany had to be set up. The London conference resolved to instruct the leaders of the German Länder to call together a constituent assembly on the basis of a popular vote. This instruction was conveyed to the German Land Presidents at a conference of the Foreign Ministers of the western powers on 1 July. The intention was that the assembly should form the basis of the parliamentary council as the constituent body of a federated Republic and ultimately a new west German Republic.

But the new western currency beat the new state to it. The currency reform of 16 July 1948 was the profoundest and most far-reaching event in German history since the war. Like a magic spell it transformed the German people. Up to then, in the words of the Federal Economics Minister Ehrhard, the Germans had been "only a hotchpotch, dispirited, irresponsible collection of individuals terrified of life."

## PARTITION AND CURRENCY REFORM

The currency reform could only succeed if it was really possible to use the new money, that is, if there were goods to spend the money on. The bold initiative of introducing the D-Mark was a success because there were still sufficient goods in the country which had been hoarded, concealed and withdrawn from public trading. These stocks, which were surprisingly large, came out into the open when the new money appeared.

Equally bold was the abolition of the controlled economy, an undertaking directed against "institutionalised poverty." It was a brave step because wide areas of the German people were kept from starvation by means of the ration card, not by money, which could buy nothing. The currency reform could only be a success if the new money was recognised as legal tender, if there was no other means of exchange in competition with the new money, neither the ration card nor the docket, which had come to be regarded as a kind of valid currency alongside the Reichsmark. It was Ludwig Ehrhard who carried through this policy with unshakeable resolve and remorseless severity; and the name of Ehrhard remains a symbol for this transformation of the German economy which has been dubbed the "Wirtschaftswunder" (economic miracle).

The creation of the D-Mark gave the Russians a new excuse for making a grab at Berlin, and this time their methods were extreme. Their aim was nothing less than cutting the lines of communication to the city, subjecting it to a blockade which would starve the city into submission and bring it under the control of the Soviet power bloc. The Soviet logic was simple but terrible: the city of Berlin was situated in the territory of the Soviet zone of occupation; therefore it belonged to the zone, come what may.

The Soviet régime immediately accused the western powers of bringing about the economic and therefore the political partition of Germany by the introduction of this divisive currency. In so doing they had destroyed the four-power government by the Allies which gave them the right to maintain troops in Berlin and use traffic routes through the Soviet zone of occupation. "The city is an island in the Soviet zone, surrounded by its territory, to which it belongs on geographical, social and historical grounds." All this was ideological covering fire for the Soviet attempt to bring Berlin into the eastern bloc by incorporating it into the currency area of the "Ostmark." But the currency reform in the Soviet zone was not technically sound; it lacked quiet preparation and thorough planning. Nor were there any hoarders and people in possession of goods who had secretly maintained illegal stocks and who were now using them to make the currency reform in west Germany a real going concern. These people, who for years had traded in contravention of the law but who were now indispensable to the success of the currency reform, were branded in the Soviet zone as "racketeers, speculators and scavengers of the black market." In contrast to west Germany, the authorities and the nationalised concerns were able to exchange their money at parity rate. The state prospered; its citizens became poorer.

The struggle between the western and eastern Mark gave perhaps the clearest illustration of the "great divide" between the two halves of Germany. The differences in standard of living and economic strength have played a significant part in intensifying the conflict between the two Germanies and in the introduction and maintenance of the oppressive laws of a closed society. For as long as the eastern half of Germany remained an impoverished zone and west Germany was an area of almost unlimited prosperity, it was inevitable that a flood of men and women should pour across the boundary between the two Germanies once the barriers were removed that made the GDR citizen a prisoner in his own country.

The Soviet offensive failed. The commandants of the western sectors declared that the Soviet orders relating to the introduction of the Ostmark into Greater Berlin were null and void.

The struggle for Berlin, which was now reaching a dramatic climax in the years 1948 and 1949, was also decisive in the struggle for Germany.

The battle of the German currencies had brought out into the open just how vast the gulf between the two Germanies really was. The currency dispute also put an end to German unity which up to then had still just been kept going by the control commission. This nominal government of Germany by the four military commanders had continued to hold Germany loosely together. And now it fell apart. The last vestige of all-German rule ceased to exist.

On 20 March 1948 the last session of the control commission took place, in a form which was scarcely friendly or pleasant. It was up to the Soviet representative to arrange the next meeting. But to this day it has not been called together. Technically it still exists, the flags still flutter outside the administrative building; but the patient is dead.

It was in March that the Russians first introduced restrictions on traffic. These were reinforced from 19 June, and little by little Berlin was sealed off. After a brief delay the western powers resolved not to give in but to remain in Berlin. It was the commander of the

American forces in Europe who was the most insistent that they should not yield one inch.

> We have lost Czechoslovakia. Norway is in great danger. If we give up Berlin and Berlin falls, west Germany will be next. If it is our intent to preserve Europe from Communism, we must stay where we are.

If it was only a matter of the kind of case that could be made, then the Soviet Union could perhaps be regarded as the champion of a nobler cause than the USA in the battle for Berlin. The Russians stressed that Berlin was part and parcel of a wider natural geographical setting. The USA note explained that the presence of American troops in Berlin did not depend on the city's four power status but on the unconditional surrender of Germany. What the USA could have said was that they were in Berlin in defence of freedom. But what they were actually saying was that they justified their presence in Berlin as victors by force of arms. The struggle for Germany continued to be darkened by the fact that all too many accommodations within and around Germany rested entirely on the fact of victory in war.

For the time being the USA was avoiding the terrible choice between giving in and handing Berlin over to the Russians on the one hand and war on the other. If Berlin had been starved into submission there would have been only two alternatives: either the USA, to their eternal humiliation, would see Berlin falling into the hands of the Russians, or they would seek to loosen the stranglehold on the city by threatening war. There was a short-term third alternative: breaking the Soviet blockade by an air lift, using American giant bombers to supply the city. Stalin had placed his hopes on a winter of starvation, but Berlin stood firm.

Perhaps the blockade would have eventually worn down Berlin's resistance. And so the USA made a disguised threat of war. On the orders of the American president Truman the B29 "atom bombers" were transferred to England. Forrestal, the American Secretary of State for War, wrote in this context that the B29s were known as the atom bombers throughout the world, and moving large numbers of them to British airfields meant that they were being brought within striking distance of Moscow. The Russians were determined to employ every "forceful means short of war" against Berlin. But in June 1949 an agreement between the western powers and the Soviet Union brought the Berlin blockade to an end. It was a renewed victory for the *status quo*: the Russians had failed in their attempt to force Berlin out of the western sphere of interest. On the other hand, there was no means open of extracting new arrangements for Berlin from the Russians which would have given peace and security to this city which had just escaped conflagration. Meanwhile the Federal Republic had been born. It had come into existence as a result of the division of Germany which had reached such a grotesque climax in the Berlin blockade. As has already been mentioned, the military governors had proposed in June 1948 to the west German Land Presidents that a constituent assembly be established on the basis of general elections. But the Presidents wanted to have nothing to do with general elections or constituent assemblies. What they proposed was that a "parliamentary council," a parliamentary body, should work out a constitution for west Germany. There is no truth in the assertion that the fires of democratic passion and the flame of self-assurance in the making of the basic law could not be kindled because the occupying powers had inhibited the development of democracy in Germany. On the contrary, the military administrations were shocked at the reservations expressed by the Presidents of the west German Länder at the introduction of a democratic assembly. The commander-in-chief of the United States Army, Clay, accused German politicians of letting fear of the Russians frighten them out of open commitment to the concept of a free society.

There was no indication that the Germans were swept along on a tide of joyous emotion at the prospect of being able to vote as a free nation once again and having free control over their own destiny. They felt less joy over the new state than grief at the loss of the old fatherland out of which they had aspired to flee into a new land. They had to guard against the voice of their own consciences accusing them of betrayal.

So the constitution of the Federal Republic lacked "self-recognition" as a conscious act of will on the part of its creators. The Federal Republic, which had refrained from recognising the GDR, only later came to full self-recognition.

When the Federal Republic was established the Germans ceased to live simply in hope, postponing all decisions until a united Germany came into being again.

The Federal Republic regarded itself as a partial reinstitution of the Reich. The victorious powers had sought the destruction of the Reich. And yet German constitutional lawyers, almost to a man, were maintaining that it had not been destroyed, that Germany still existed. Whatever forms of state might emerge in Germany they would in a special and subtle way be linked with the old German Reich as it existed between 1871 and 1933, and carry the same responsibilities as it bore, perhaps too its guilt and its rights.

There are two schools of thought as far as the state and the law are concerned, one of which insists that the Reich is dead, the other regards the continued existence of the Reich as both an historical and a legal fact and as a political and moral obligation.

Such an exceptional event as the destruction of an empire can at any rate not be comprehended in terms of outdated legal concepts. The GDR has nothing but scorn for such a concept of the reconstruction of the state in Germany. The Reich is dead and gone, but the nation lives on; that was the immediate reaction at the time when the SED was still a proponent of the idea of a single nation. The next step was a retreat from the concept of national unity. During this phase all the blame for the collapse of Germany was laid at the door of west German imperialism. Finally the SED adopted Khrushchev's two-state theory: Germany lies in ruins, it is dead, nothing remains of it. The dead will not come back again, and because the dead do not return the old Germany must be destroyed root and branch.

The foundation of the Federal Republic was Adenauer's finest hour. Up until then he had been a second-rank figure, but by giving the Federal Republic world status he became a man of international standing.

Adenauer left his mark on the German question; he gave it a meaning all of its own and developed it into a leading factor in the international struggle against the Soviet Union. In his eyes Bolshevism signified the manifestation of evil in the guise of a state, godlessness assuming the form of a political party. For a long time he kept alive in Germany and in the world at large a belief in a long-term threat from the east.

But he was not one of those people who kicked out against the fact of defeat; he was one of those rare figures in Germany, a man with no trace of hysteria, with no dreams of national greatness. The pathos of national glory rebounded off him. For many years he was the very embodiment of the Federal Republic. He also represented the sobering down of the German nation. In the Federal Republic under Konrad Adenauer there was no sign of the hectic toing and froing of the Weimar Republic. All forms of radicalism had faded away. Alongside the economic miracle a political miracle occurred: the Germans did not rise up in a frenzy of nationalism. It was a shattered, fragmented nation, one in which 10 million people had lost their homes and means of subsistence, and millions more had suffered the pain and humiliations of being prisoners of war; a nation which had starved until 1949; a country in which work had been meaningless until the currency reform. But in contrast to 1918 the German people were all too conscious of the fact of their defeat in 1945. This time they had been truly broken. No longer could anyone maintain that the other side had not won an indisputable victory, nor that they might have won if they had played their hand a little better and the cards had been on their side. Adenauer's policy was founded upon resignation.

His first objective was to bring order to one part of Germany which he regarded as healthy, to fashion it into the nucleus to which the rest of Germany could attach itself at a later date. He regarded this as a necessary detour on the road towards reuniting the country and he took the view that the detour would be a short one. For a long time he cherished the illusion that a west Germany utterly immune against Communism would convince the Russians of the hopelessness of their efforts towards making the whole of Germany Bolshevist. He failed to recognise that those in power "on the other side" might be quite satisfied with their part of Germany, in the same way that he, Konrad Adenauer, was for the time being content with his. At that time it seemed that the Russian zone could never rise up again out of its wretched condition in which the population scarcely had the bare minimum of existence. At that time freedom seemed powerful enough to force repression to retreat little by little. But the historical significance of Adenauer lies above all else in the fact that, in the words of Herbert Wehner, "he stood for something," a focal point of political order and power. He took a decision that broke with centuries of German history. He put an end to the oscillations of German policy between east and west, and shattered the illusion that Germany did not have to choose between east and west and could play one off against the other.

In the political philosophy of Joseph Wirth, who was Chancellor between 1921 and 1922, the Treaty of Locarno (of friendship with the west) could take its place alongside a secret treaty between the Reich army and the Red Army. Adenauer, on the other hand, held firmly to the basic principle that the Federal Republic had to nail its colours to the western mast for better or for worse. As a tactician of great cunning Adenauer worked on simple principles which he seemed to follow with an all but naive directness. He had put his shirt on co-operation with the western powers, and especially with the USA. He became their staunch ally—but only after very tough bargaining behind closed doors.

In a moment of bitterness, Kurt Schumacher, the leader of the Social Democrats, branded him as the "Chancellor of the Allies." And indeed Adenauer put his signature to the most ridiculous documents, with pious and devout duplicity. He placed his faith in the passage of time and the "dynamism of events" which would leave all these treaties far behind, and in the main he was proved right. In one of his speeches Churchill had said that if Germany and France were friends anything would be possible in Europe, but if they were not, nothing would be possible. The stages in this rapprochement were the Schumann Plan, the merging of the French and German mining industries, and finally the Common Market. Adenauer's chief opponent, Kurt Schumacher, accused

* *

him of putting Europe before Germany. But when the victorious powers came together to bring the Federal Republic into being the USA was baptising a new Europe. In a speech at Harvard University, the USA Foreign Minister, Marshall, put forward the plan which was to bear his name: a loan of 800 million dollars was to put a stop to the breakdown of the European economy, because there was no doubt that the European economy would fall into the hands of the Communists if the plight of Europe continued unchecked. But a European economic union would have to be set up, he argued, to prevent this economic aid from being frittered away and to permit it to bear full fruit in the context of Europe as a whole and under the auspices of a comprehensive plan. Konrad Adenauer led the Federal Republic to the Common Market as its firstborn son, and there is no doubt that the Federal Republic derived by far the greatest profit from the Marshall Plan. European economic unity and a genuine political rapprochement in Europe took longer to develop than many people had hoped. Adenauer only saw the beginnings of a true European community.

The Marshall Plan led to a crucial decision in American policy whose real significance for the course of German history can scarcely be recognised even now. General Marshall, and General Wendelmeier, whom he had sent out as an observer, persuaded President Truman at the time that it was beyond the power of the USA to set up in addition to the European aid programme a similar gigantic scheme which would also hold back Asian Communism. There followed the victory of Mao in China, and this brought in its train all those upheavals in Asia whose effects continue to be felt until the present day.

It was a similar tragedy to that of 1918. Then there was no success in putting an end to war once and for all and in making the world safe for democracy, because it is not exactly easy to persuade nations to make even a fraction of the sacrifices in peacetime that they had in war. A tiny proportion of the efforts which all the nations had made in the two wars would have been more than enough to ensure the establishment of international peace and the predominance of democracy throughout the world. The Weimar Republic had collapsed simply and solely because it had not been established in the context of an international order founded upon peace and democracy. Hitler would have been an impossibility in a world "safe for democrats to live in."

All those elements of uncertainty and danger inherent in German history since 1945 can again be traced back to the fact that there is still no peace in our time and that those world powers whose obligation it was to serve as guardians of peace and democracy in Germany are not the unchallenged leading powers of the world. In

1945 they won the war again, but lost the peace. After the Second World War as after the First, the world was still not safe for democracy. A world system in which the democracies can feel utterly secure has yet to come into being. Thus it is that in the most recent years of German history the Germans have experienced a vague sense of unease in the face of the Vietnam war.

Once more the shadow of a lost peace lay across German history. The war did not end for the Germans with a peace treaty. In the thousand years of their history the German people have seldom experienced real peace.

The Federal Republic was bound to the west for all time from the time when Chancellor Adenauer decided to rearm the Republic. The generous plan of a "European army" foundered when the French national assembly voted it out. The European army would have rendered integration and intermingling of the nations possible to such a degree that German and French soldiers would have found themselves side by side in the trenches as comrades in arms.

Finally the Federal Republic was brought into NATO. The Federal army with its twelve divisions belongs to some extent at least to NATO, because of all the armies of the western powers it alone is completely under the orders of NATO down to the last soldier and the last general.

On the other side of the fence, the GDR is a member of the Warsaw Pact, the eastern equivalent of NATO. This has rendered both west Germany and the GDR once and for all time utterly unfitted to form part of a united Germany. How will it ever be possible for these two Germanies ever to come together again for as long as they are members of opposing military blocs?

The rearmament of the Federal Republic has come under the shadow of that misunderstood and misleading term : power politics. The western military bloc has never been so powerful that it could go on to the offensive. But the western military system was sufficient to prevent the Soviet Union from advancing beyond its side of the iron curtain. Power politics has allowed the Federal Republic to survive, no more and no less. Rearmament on both sides of the iron curtain reinforced the *status quo*, on the one side western freedom, on the other, western impotence. It seems a long time since the two young Germanies in their first tender years have been threatened from undermining from within. For many years the Soviet Union has sought in vain to stir up revolutionary movements in western Europe with whose help the whole of Europe could be turned Communist.

All these movements came to nothing. The west for its part had tried to support liberal and anti-Communist movements in eastern Europe; but these were bloodily suppressed without exception. The

Communist powers of eastern Europe employed the hangman to demonstrate the impotence of the west.

Above all it seems a long time since the régime of the Soviet zone seemed corrupt and weak enough to be done away with overnight. It seemed obvious that freedom could easily overcome a tyranny of prisons and concentration camps. The other states of the eastern bloc—Poland, Hungary, Czechoslovakia, Rumania, Bulgaria—have all achieved national unity under Communist domination, have gained a foothold in the industrial revolution and taken their share of technical progress. But the foundation of the GDR is fatefully bound up with the destruction of Germany's national unity. What was the sense of a kind of Communism in Saxony, whose aim was industrial revolution, when Saxony was in the forefront of European industrial development?

But the early sufferings of this country are not entirely—and perhaps even not principally—the responsibility of the Communist régime which, in Stalin's phrase, fitted a country like Germany like a saddle on a cow.

During Soviet occupation the zone had been plundered systematically enough. The Federal Republic had been fortunate in its victors. The US soldiers had lacked for nothing during the invasion of Germany. If the population of the conquered country were starving, the soldiers who were conquering them were certainly not. In the east of Germany, however, the soldiers were just as short of food as the defeated population, and the hungry simply stole from the starving. The eastern half of Germany found itself chained to a victorious power which was itself beaten and exhausted. The victorious powers had agreed that each of the occupying powers should exact reparations from their own zone. The Russians all but bled their zone to death for many years after the war.

For a long time theirs was a zone of suffering in which the population was only able to keep body and soul together with the utmost exertions. The two events which stand out from the grey uniformity of its history after 1945, the uprising of 17 June 1953 and the building of the wall, are evidence of the great and terrible deprivations of eastern Germany. Right up until 1962 the GDR was Stalinist in the worst sense of the term. Industrial life consisted of persistent extortion of levy to Russia. All too often it served as the whip—almost literally—which was the only thing that kept working life going in the zone. The uprising of 17 June 1953 broke out because the levy payable by building workers was to be raised and because the régime's irresolution in the face of the striking workers was taken by the mass of the population as evidence that the Ulbricht system was in a state of collapse and that Moscow was giving up the domination of the SED. In a few hours the streets were thronged with noisy crowds. The régime crumpled as if it had been struck a physical blow. Not one of the state police lifted a hand in its defence. But then the Soviet High Command called in the tanks, and in a few hours it was all over. The Soviet army did not have to fire a single shot, and their conduct on that day was most honourable.

The young men who threw stones at the Soviet tanks epitomised the touching impotence and idealistic folly of the whole enterprise. No leadership came into being, there was no visible purpose or practical objective in the swirling masses of people driven by their anger and sufferings. There was no delegate body to take the first essential step, without which the uprising would inevitably be scattered like chaff in the wind, and that was to explain to the Russians that the uprising was not directed against them. It became evident to the world at large on that June day in 1953 that the régime in the Russian zone was not to be toppled by such means. And equally it became clear to those in power in the zone that they could not possibly allow free elections to take place for many a long year.

The sufferings in the zone were for a long time so severe that serious observers ventured the opinion that the régime would dwindle away to nothing, because its population was gradually slipping away out of its hands, and the zone would simply die away. Up until very recently it was the only country in which the population was steadily decreasing. Death comes more quickly than life.

The population of the zone flooded out like water from a burst dam, year after year, with little opposition on the part of the régime. The zone permitted this emigration to take place because it was not yet capable of offering food and work to its own population. In 1961 the tide of refugees rose so high that it seemed the entire populace were fleeing the zone. It was now a matter of life and death for the GDR; but the means the GDR chose among the many possible alternatives of meeting the danger was in the nature of a challenge: the construction of the wall which sliced Berlin in half, dividing a once proud city like a cattle grid across the middle of a banqueting hall.

But the wall served its purpose. For the GDR it signified an obligation to intensify economic reconstruction and raise the standard of living. From the GDR side the erection of the wall meant that the country was announcing to the world its intention to stand on its own feet. Since that time the work of reconstruction has advanced to such an extent that the barrier has become superfluous. The notion—which for a while formed the basis of reunification policy in the west—that the GDR was destined to crumble in ruins and that it was only being held together by brute force has taken a long time to disappear from western thought. The Germany on the other side of the iron curtain also stopped regarding itself as little more than a transitional state and a springboard to a Germany united under Communist rule.

Khrushchev, Stalin's successor, expressed it like this: there was no longer any question of a united Germany, not even one brought together under a revolutionary banner. Khrushchev proposed the notion of two Germanies. As a result of the war Germany had split into two states, each having its own independence and sovereignty under international law. There was no longer any such thing as a German Reich.

But, as Willy Brandt was later to stress as Chancellor of the Federal Republic, the German nation still existed, and this was at a time when the Federal Republic had finally come to acknowledge its own long-term existence. But in fact two German states had risen up; the foundation of the Federal Republic—like that of the GDR—was in the moment of its coming into being not the first step towards a new "Germany," but a move in the opposite direction. As soon as it became evident that neither of these Germanies could either brush aside or absorb the other, it became equally clear that any new all-German community would only be able to emerge with the consent of the two German states. As far as the idea of one Germany was concerned, Adenauer's policy, even at its most successful, was doomed to ultimate failure.

As early as the fifties it was clear that the existence of the two Germanies was an unpleasant fact of life. In accordance with a long-standing Russian tradition, the Soviet Union turned the division of Germany to its own advantage. Slowly and painfully the GDR rose up out of the former misery which had seemed to brand it as an unviable freak. The Federal Republic, favoured by circumstances in a whole variety of ways, progressed by leaps and bounds; but now the GDR too was making considerable advances in the work of reconstruction. The reign of terror in the eastern zone began to pass, although it took the masters of the GDR a long time to realise that their state did not need to resort to inhumanity in order to maintain itself.

The contrast between the two German states was no longer characterised by prosperity on the one side and starvation on the other, and a deadly enmity between the two Germanies could no longer be regarded as an inevitable historical necessity. The cold war had given place to peaceful coexistence—and this change has been universally welcomed. But such shifts in attitude are more verbal than practical in nature, a cover on the part of both

Germanies for the fact that they did not really want to progress any further than coexistence.

On the whole coexistence was the guiding principle in relations between the Federal Republic and the GDR, although the opposite has often seemed to be the case. Up to now the crises have turned out to be minor skirmishes: each time after the dust had settled, the shape of Germany and Europe at large has become more firmly fixed on the lines of the war map of 1945 which were originally traced with the sword. These boundaries have proven unshakeable and impregnable and have never really been challenged.

Rigid attitudes became more flexible. The habit of staring straight through one another gradually died away, not because the basic outline of Europe was shifting, but because it was becoming stabilised.

One factor has posed a long-standing threat to coexistence: Berlin. The continuing existence of West Berlin has constituted a stumbling-block to any progress towards normalising relations and stabilising the frontiers between the two Germanies. The Soviet Union and the GDR have consistently regarded West Berlin as a thorn in the flesh and an enemy fortress deep within their own territory. On the other side of the coin, they inevitably regarded this "island in the Red Sea" as a bastion under siege, as a prize which they would surely capture in the long run. They have tried time and again to lay their hands on West Berlin and will only loosen their stranglehold on the city when they think they can step back to strike the death-blow.

The battle for Berlin, which reached its tense climax in 1948, marked the great watershed for Germany.

In October 1958, after a period of apparent quiet, the Russians risked their hand again. They announced—using Walter Ulbricht as their mouthpiece—that the whole of Berlin lay within the boundaries of the GDR, and the whole of Berlin belonged to her sovereign territory, and on 27 November 1958 the Soviet Union delivered its "ultimatum" on the Berlin question. The Soviet note stated that "in the historical capital of Germany two vastly different worlds rub shoulders, and all around the barricades of the cold war rise up. In its present state, Berlin is nothing less than 'a lighted fuse'." In fact it was Soviet policy that had made Berlin the fuse on the powder keg.

What the Soviet note says about Berlin being a "front-line city" is true. But Berlin also represents the front line of the free world where the battle for the fate of Germany is fought. It is the front line where the fight is on to decide whether "Germany" will continue to have any history. The diplomatic notes went back and forth. The cloud of uncertainty dissipated when it became clear that war would result if Berlin were taken by force. In the end the battle for Berlin got nowhere. The Russians had failed in their attempt to break up from within the power system which had existed since 1945 by the annexation of Berlin.

Only gradually did the two German states come to like the idea of becoming separate entities. After 1948 the Presidents of the Länder had rejected the proposal of the military governors that the German constitution should be decided upon by a constituent assembly. To the German statesmen such a step seemed to bestow too much solemnity and dignity on the newly independent west German state. It was only with the greatest hesitancy that the Germans moved along the path that led to separatism. Incredulous at what was happening, they tried to resist, but they were driven along against their will, torn away from the Germany which had been their mother country.

An undivided Germany could not break free from its misery, and the reforms which would bring Germany out of the depths could only be initiated by the western side or the eastern side acting independently. The only way in which the Germans could hope to save themselves from destruction and social and economic oblivion was by partition. Germany had to divide itself, in order to survive. The two Germanies were born of the mutual hatred of the victorious powers. Because their unity collapsed the Germans rose up again from their wretchedness and ruination, but "Germany" was lost. Even when the Bonn constitution was being drawn up the question was still undecided as to whether the Reich continued to exist or whether Germany after defeat was "potter's clay" in the hands of its new masters, which they could fashion as they pleased.

The Germans hoped that a new era in their history was beginning when Stalin, the man who had so ruthlessly intervened in German history, died. Stalin had said at the Potsdam conference that "Germany is what is left of the country." In the middle of 1956 Khrushchev, Stalin's successor, had pilloried his predecessor in a shock speech. This event is certainly without historical parallel. Revolutions have always devoured their own offspring, but this time a revolution was eating its own dead. And now the Germans were hoping that the Soviet state would cancel out all that Stalin's German policy had wrought. But after Stalin Russian policy towards Germany became harder and even more inhuman than in his time. The new masters of the Soviet Union intensified the division of Germany by compelling the Federal Republic to recognise them. What a strange situation it was to find that the Federal Republic feared recognition by a world power as a dangerous burden. Other new states invariably welcome recognition of this kind. But Soviet recognition of the Federal Republic amounted to a public pronouncement that there were two German states. The Federal Republic was to be compelled to give formal recognition of the fact of its existence as a separate German state. Russia had returned to its long-standing policy of neutralising Germany by setting two German states up in opposition. The Soviet Union held a trump card: the German prisoners-of-war which it still held. The blackmail was conducted in a subtle and elusive manner, because the Soviet Union had been claiming that there were no prisoners of war any more, only war criminals sentenced by Soviet courts to forced labour. In this way one and a half million Germans had been turned into "war criminals" by show trials. And so the Moscow treaty between the Federal Republic and the Soviet Union was concluded without the prisoners of war even receiving a mention. The negotiations in Moscow were an impressive example of grand diplomacy in which both parties rose to the occasion and defended their cause with an unblemished conscience. The Russians began the negotiations by declaring that due account had to be taken of those two facts of life that went by the name of the Federal Republic and the GDR. There was little point in Adenauer's question in reply: "What are the realities of the situation? Germany or partition? The division of Germany is unnatural. It runs counter to divine law and human rights. I can see no useful purpose in speaking about it in terms of realities. There will be no real security in Europe unless and until Germany is reunified." When Adenauer demanded the release of German prisoners of war, the Soviet leader Bulganin replied that there were only German war criminals still left in the Soviet Union, and they had been sentenced by Russian courts. "Those are individuals bereft of humanity, men of violence, arsonists, the murderers of women, old men and children." In the end, just as Adenauer was about to leave, agreement was reached. The Federal Republic declared its readiness to open diplomatic relations, and the Russian politicians gave a verbal promise that they would release the German prisoners of war. Adenauer gave evidence of his considerable stature as a statesman by taking the Bolshevists at their word of honour, despite what his entourage had to say about Soviet duplicity.

The social patterns and the decision taken on either side of the zonal frontier became more and more final. Only in one case did it seem that the "temporary" state of things was done away with: on 23 October 1955 68 per cent of the electorate of the Saar rejected the "European Statute for the Saar" which claimed to be offering a "European solution" of the Saar question and which sought to set up a long-term "transitional" settlement. Even the German Chancellor's signature stood at the bottom of this "European Statute." But the Germans took the view that they no longer needed to resort to the tortuous dealings with which Konrad Adenauer advanced the German cause in the face of defeat and international dangers. It is true that Konrad Adenauer himself believed in his heart that the Saar question would have to find its own natural outcome one day, namely by reuniting the Germans in the Saarland with Germany; but, like Stresemann, he was playing it too subtly. In the Saar "Germany" now seemed to have emerged victorious. Many took the view that the way the voting went in the Saar would have set an excellent example for reuniting Germany in peace and freedom. The Saar had repeatedly changed its masters: in 1815, 1918, 1935, 1945 and now in 1955, and Germany had always exercised great attraction on the people of the Saar when the Reich was powerful. They are, in the words of a French thinker, "like flowers which in the morning turn their faces towards the rising sun." In fact the settlement of the Saar question, this final solution of a centuries-old problem, has demonstrated the folly of the German war with the west. The Saar question proved that there was no single issue between Germany and the rest which could justify enmity and war. For long periods of German history there only seemed to be "movement" in the east; but here too for a while there was peace. Even the great upheavals in eastern Europe—the German uprising of 17 June, the "October" in Poland which liberated the Polish state from extremely oppressive dependence on the Soviet Union, the uprising in Hungary bloodily crushed by Soviet tanks, the "Spring" in Czechoslovakia and the military occupation of the country by the Soviet army—brought no modifications to the 1945 "wartime map" and only served to reinforce its demarcation lines more cruelly than had been done when hostilities ceased. The Soviet Union made it unambiguously clear in all these events that it was the Russian intention to hold fast on to the territories gained in the Second World War. And "its" Germany counted as one of those possessions, and the Russians also laid claim to Berlin which had come into the Russian sphere of influence as a result of the confussion of events after 1945.

On 25 March 1957 Adenauer seemed to be bringing home the harvest of his European policy; for this was the day on which the Rome Treaty of the European Economic Community was signed. Since then some movement in the direction of economic integration in Europe has taken place. And this certainly has a wider political significance; for the involvement of the Federal Republic with the economy of America and western Europe has reached such a level that any unilateral military adventure on the part of the Federal Republic would inevitably lead to solitary suicide.

# THE ECONOMIC MIRACLE: RECONCILIATION WITH FRANCE AND THE *SPIEGEL* AFFAIR

The policy of oscillation between east and west was finished for good. The Federal Republic is bound to the west for better or for worse. But it is only half of Germany which is integrated with half of Europe. The fact that Europe and Germany have been involved in a terrible conflict has hung like a shadow over Germany in the past decades.

The guidelines for German history in the years after the war had been set when the Germans were confronted with the choice between continuing to remain in chaos and misery, waiting for the day of reunification to come, or beginning the work of reconstruction in two different German states with quite distinct modes of life. Economic prosperity became and remained the hallmark of the Federal Republic. It is a strange fact, and one that casts a curious light on the events of recent years, that it should be the German people who should experience the greatest economic boom for a century, and after such a shattering defeat in war.

After the currency reform and the Marshall Plan the defeated nation became the richest nation in Europe. The Allies had sworn not to repeat the mistake of 1918 by taking away obsolete machinery from Germany as war reparations, and then giving them the money to buy the latest and most up to date equipment in the world. But after 1945 the Germans were able to establish the most modern economy in the world, because from a social and economic standpoint they had been obliged to start off from square one.

Over the last decades the Federal Republic has become the most politically and economically stable country in the world. The "economic miracle" was perhaps not miraculous, but it was something of a mystery. And on top of that a political miracle happened: in a nation which had just emerged from the uttermost wretchedness, all forms of radicalism vanished into empty air. It was as if the earth had opened and swallowed up the Communists and National Socialists who in the March elections in 1933 were able to command 22 million votes. "Bonn is not Weimar" ran the catchphrase which sought to illuminate this mystifying transformation of an entire nation. Throughout the whole period of its existence the Weimar Republic had been shaken by a succession of passions, fanatical outbursts and epileptic fits. And now there appeared a republic based on Bonn free of destructive passions, rational, sober, a model of stability, a country without strikes and up until the fall of the Erhard government almost without government crises. There was scarcely a breath of wind until people began to be afraid of this very stillness itself, and in the student troubles of 1967 thunderclouds appeared on the horizon of this exemplary republic. At the Geneva summit conference in 1956 a Russian diplomat said: "In Germany the sons always rise up against their father; in five, ten or fifteen years everything in Germany that now exists will be cursed and rejected."

It seemed that he was right: sons do revolt against their fathers and no one knows whether the passage of a few years will see the condemnation of all that has hitherto been held to be the fundamental principles and golden rules of the Federal Republic. But for the most part the rebels against the welfare state are themselves impregnated with the spirit of the welfare society. They see before them a country drenched in an almost magic rain of riches and they are tired of the difficult path that leads them there. The young people's rebellion has had an unexpected measure of success—the establishment seemed to cower back as if before a ghost from the past—simply because in an imperfect world any revolution can find plenty of things which need change, reform and almost revolutionary measures. But the country as a whole was not fired by the enthusiasm of the young, particularly in the universities, because there were no longer people in Germany who had nothing to lose but their chains, and because the classes where in the twentieth century revolution has originated—workers, peasants and soldiers—no longer represent even the remotest threat to German stability.

For a long time the Germans have revealed themselves as a sobered nation, tired of intoxicating ideals, the slogans of greatness, and the dangers of power. But in the so-called "Spiegel affair" the Federal Republic was once more suddenly threatened by dangers similar to those of the not too distant past. In the Federal Republic there was opposition among journalists, a campaign waged by a small group which exercised a disproportionately large influence in the main media influencing public opinion: radio, press and television. It caused Adenauer all the more annoyance because in his eyes it became suspect on grounds of ideological self-righteousness and subtle hyper-intelligence. The weekly journal *Der Spiegel* appeared to be representative of this opposition and was striking a new note in political journalism. The Federal Republic was experiencing its first political crisis as the government sought to rid itself of this inconvenient critic. They did not create the *Spiegel* affair, but they exploited it.

It was sparked off when the government gave its full support to a charge of treason which the Federal legal authorities had taken up against *Der Spiegel* on their own initiative. The cause was an article by Conrad Ahlers "Immediate defence readiness" which was a critical account of the NATO manoeuvre "Fallex." Ahlers was supported by German and foreign army men who were opposed to the strategic views of Federal Minister of Defence Strauss. It is certain that the article did not tell the Russian general staff anything they did not know already. The legal authorities and an extremely heated Adenauer rose to the heights of stupidity by putting the editors and publishers of *Der Spiegel* on the same level as those pitiable creatures who betray their country for money.

> Now, ladies and gentlemen, we stand before an abyss of treason in our country. For, when treason is systematically committed, ladies and gentlemen, by a paper with a circulation of half a million copies, in order to make money. . . .

If that were true, and only if it were true, then the Federal government would have been entitled to do what they did and more besides. A passing knowledge of the personalities involved would have been more than enough to convince them that this was not so. A small effort to obtain information would have spared Adenauer from having his image tarnished by an accusation which was as laughable as it was utterly inexcusable. It very rarely happened that Adenauer allowed hatred to overcome reason and justice.

This fixation upon the idea that here was a case of underhand, paid treason raised the affair to the level of a German Dreyfus case. The action caused such an uproar, cost so much money, and took place with such indecent haste as if some great conspiracy against the Federal Republic was being confronted, as if delay would have placed the Republic in the gravest danger. Even inside the Bonn government itself people were finding Russians under the bed; this was why the Federal Minister of Justice himself was not informed. Columns of police roared out, moving in on the *Spiegel* building in Hamburg like an entire army, and arrests and searches in the middle of the night brought back memories of the Third Reich.

Adenauer was tormented by the prospect that Conrad Ahlers—who was in Madrid and according to a statement by the Chancellor in possession of a visa for Tangiers—would go to ground in North Africa. So Strauss, the Federal Minister of Defence, telephoned the German military attaché Oster in Madrid and gave him the task of having Ahlers arrested. It would not have been all that surprising if the order had been to bring him in dead or alive. And the Spanish police were more than co-operative. They ensured that the Federal Republic could get their hands on this dangerous individual, but in such a way that any action which might in any way be outside the law was left to their German colleagues; they did not do the arresting, they only expelled Ahlers, but not without getting him to state in writing that they had done nothing of the sort.

In the Federal parliament Franz-Josef Strauss denied that he had anything to do with Ahlers' arrest. The German public was too incensed to lend credit to his statement that all he intended to say was that he had nothing to do with the institution of proceedings against the *Spiegel.* Strauss was accused of lying to parliament, but that did not rouse Adenauer at first. It was only when Strauss told the truth—that the Chancellor had been the guiding force behind the whole affair—that Adenauer let him fall.

Throughout the Republic fear was rife in both camps. The state seemed threatened by dark dangers. In his own words, the historian Gerhard Ritter felt his face flush with anger "when a bunch of journalists of the greatest cunning" reported on a matter which he regarded as a state secret. As in early 1933, he was overwhelmed by "the sensation of standing on a landslide which was moving towards the cliff edge." On the other side of the coin, the mass of the people nearly rose up in rebellion because they scented dark forces behind the action against *Der Spiegel,* an authoritarian power which set itself above the rights of freedom and free expression.

The affair brought discredit on the government. "An abyss of treachery" and not one single conviction. But the government did not fall because of such a monstrous and frivolously-brought accusation, even though Adenauer did not emerge unscathed from the affair. Franz-Josef Strauss, accused of deceiving parliament, became a minister again after a couple of years.

The shadows grew longer. Konrad Adenauer was no longer in full command of the course of political events. In international circles he no longer gained the same kind of response as before, because the world at large no longer feared the Soviet Union so greatly, nor did others believe as he did, that war was a constant threat.

Adenauer felt that the foreign policy of the Federal Republic was beginning to lose its impetus and become ineffective. In 1962 he sought once more to take the initiative in a big way and influence the future direction of international politics by entering into a peace treaty with France. As he understood it, European problems centred on a reconciliation between France and Germany. In his eyes this was the fulfilment of European, French and German history. Winston Churchill had voiced similar sentiments in a speech at Fulton, in which he had spoken for a holy alliance of the European nations. In his view, nothing was possible if France and Germany remained enemies; everything possible if they became friends.

President de Gaulle in his German visit of September 1962 gave the German people a more significant and all-embracing task than any German statesman had ventured to do:

> I congratulate you on being young Germans, that is to say, children of a great nation. Yes, a great nation, which in the course of its history has made great mistakes. A nation, however, equally capable of offering the world great spiritual, scientific, artistic and philosophical moments and which has enriched the world by countless products of its inventive power, its technology, and its productivity; a nation which in its work for peaceful ends, as also in the sufferings of war, has revealed enormous resources of courage, discipline and organisational capability. . . .

It was as if he had given the Germans the courage to face up to the past, to live in the knowledge of their own history. But the friendship treaty also had practical political ends. In de Gaulle's mind at least, it was a move in the direction of establishing a Europe with France and Germany as the leading powers. De Gaulle wanted France to be the strongest power in this "Europe of the nations" which he advocated. He wanted to make France a great military power once more. This was the ulterior motive in enlisting the aid of the Federal Republic and its willingness to co-operate technically and financially in the great rearmament of France. The Germans were being offered the chance of participating in the leadership of Europe, but at a price which was so high that the Republic did not pay it there and then. After a second visit de Gaulle told the German ambassador in Paris that the marriage between the Federal Republic and France had not been consummated. "Moi, je suis rentré vierge." (I have returned a virgin.)

Deep down, Adenauer did not want to have a successor while he was still alive; it was his opinion that the Federal Republic would not survive without him; he did not want to leave office and his duties until he closed his eyes for the last time. Above all he did not want to give way to Ludwig Erhard, who had been put foward as his successor by his own party. But on 12 October 1963 the first Chancellor of the Federal Republic, "the everlasting Chancellor," stepped down for good. Erhard, the man of the economic miracle, was now for the majority of Germans the man of the hour. The Federal elections of 1965 seemed to give the lie to the retiring Chancellor's prognosis that Ludwig Erhard lacked political instincts. Erhard fought the election with incredible spirit and ferocity, led his party to victory and in so doing laid the foundations for his second term of office. The election was a plebiscite in favour of the Chancellor, of prosperity and the welfare state.

On the surface at least, the period of Erhard's government was uneventful. But it too was unable to tread water on the German question as long as the parties in the Federal parliament had before them plans which sought practical alterations in the *status quo*; and so far it had occurred to no one—unlike Willy Brandt in 1970—to make recognition of the *status quo* into the starting point from which to move quietly towards overcoming it. The many agreements on passes for mutual movement across the wall were the only events that marked this otherwise uneventful time.

The government decided upon non-recognition of the new states in the east, but they were already too firmly established by far for the most passionate non-recognition to have the least effect on them. The Federal Republic acted in accordance with the law which had brought it into being, and so continued to be caught up in international political conflict. That fact is demonstrated above all else by the diplomatic recognition of Israel which was without doubt the most important event under Erhard's chancellorship. It seemed that the Federal Republic had thereby become involved in the jungle of the near east struggle for power, as it had earlier with Adenauer's agreement on reparations, and to provoke three hundred million Mohammedans the majority of whom had sworn death to this young state. But it was this very fact which compelled the Federal Republic to recognise Israel. By taking the step of recognition, the Federal Republic was saying no more and no less than that Israel had a right to exist. It was an obligation to German history to make a stand against the extinction of this country, and it inevitably took on the appearance of a macabre posthumous victory against Hitler and something to be set against the German national debt.

## THE GRAND COALITION: WHAT IS OUR ATTITUDE TO THE GDR?

Ludwig Erhard was to become a victim of his own success. The society based on prosperity which he had fathered made ever-shifting demands on its citizens. Erhard, who had once made consumer consumption his election platform, became the Chancellor who tried with total lack of success to preach moderation. His exhortations to work, to avoid foreign travel, to put the brake on consumption, fell on deaf ears. His term of office came to an end with the Federal budget in deficit. In the last analysis, Erhard's government collapsed because the FDP party leadership would have nothing to do with the compromise agreement on getting the economy back in the black accepted by the FDP ministers. So the FDP ministers left the government, and the Federal Republic at large regarded this as the Chancellor's death sentence. It was true that for a long time Erhard had been letting things slip. He was no longer regarded as a fit man to take up the reins of government again. But this was only the tip of the iceberg. Beneath the surface the Federal Republic was going through a profound economic and social crisis.

Erhard belonged to the age of Adenauer; and at times he was regarded as its miracle worker. Such was his trusting and simple faith in Adenauer's foreign policy that Adenauer began to doubt his political abilities. None the less the Erhard government had by means of a "peace plan" brought into being the formula of "non-violence" which under the next government but one was to become the basis of a treaty between the Federal Republic and the Soviet Union.

But the impression that German policies as a whole had stagnated was so strong that the general opinion was that only a government with a substantial majority would be capable of solving the great issues that lay before the nation.

The formation of the coalition from two of the larger German parties, the SPD and the CDU/CSU (Chancellor: Kiesinger; Foreign Minister and Deputy Chancellor: Brandt; Minister for All-German Affairs: Wehner; Economics Minister: Schiller; Finance Minister: Strauss; Defence Minister: Schröder), answered the necessity of the hour when the coalition between the CDU and the FDP had broken up and an alliance between the SPD and the FDP did not seem to be on the cards.

There is a distinction to be drawn between a coalition government and a national government. The former derives from difficulties in the formation of a government, which have their origins in an uncertain situation inside parliament; the latter is definable as a government of mutual co-operation when weighty national problems—such as always arise in time of war—have to be resolved and decisions taken on which the nation as a whole must speak with a single voice. The grand coalition was first conceived in terms of a national government. The expectation was that with its huge majority it would resolve the great national issues in a totally different manner from that of a lesser coalition: namely, electoral law reform, Ostpolitik, the economic crisis. But despite its majority, the grand coalition was incapable of finding answers to these questions because the two parties concerned cancelled one another out and there was hardly ever any real majority in favour of big reforms. A government compounded of two contrasting political philosophies is capable of positive policy-making only when a situation like war compels the coalition to take joint action.

It was particularly difficult to find common ground between the two parties in matters of foreign policy, for each laid stress on different aspects of the German question. It is an unalterable fact that the *status quo* cannot be changed and that a German foreign policy based on non-recognition is doomed to inaction. But it is equally true that the Germans have never felt able to accept the way things are wholeheartedly, and, in addition, that it is more than probable that a policy of recognition would work more to their advantage than mere passive acceptance. Attitudes towards the future shape of Germany are not a simple matter of black and white. There is no one overriding consideration which stands out above all others. None of the German political parties puts forward its German programme with unshakeable conviction. Each policy has its ifs and buts, and there are always reservations to be overcome whenever there is something to be done or left undone. Each of the German parties has the same bad conscience, hesitancy and discomfiture in the face of the German question. The CDU/CSU knows as well as the SPD that the pattern of states which came out of the Second World War is quite simply unalterable. On the other hand, the SPD knows as well as the CDU/CSU the pangs of conscience which every German feels at the oppression of Europeans and Germans. The chief argument of each of the parties consists in demonstration of the fact that the German policies of the other is powerless to change the status quo (whether it be recognition or non-recognition); the frightening thing about the situation is that they are both right.

But at least non-recognition had been tried already; recognition was an unknown quantity. And new approaches—which were founded upon recognition, or at least a greater degree of recognition than before—were beginning to assert themselves more and more; and in December 1966 the Federal Minister for all-German affairs, Herbert Wehner, took the same line in an interview with *Vorwärts.* The ultimate objective of this German policy line was still stated in terms of "reuniting of a divided nation." This is an obligation which the constitution places on every German government, Wehner said, but it must be recognised that immediate results should not be expected and that the process of reunification was essentially a long-term measure. It was in his view self-evident that there was no question of imposing the social patterns of the Federal Republic on to the other part of Germany, nor should there be at any stage any exploitation of the minority position of the GDR population. Those who were living in that part of Germany which had detached itself from ourselves, Wehner continued, should be permitted to make a free choice in respect of their future way of life, even if this ran counter to that chosen by the majority of the citizens of the Federal Republic. But even Wehner left open the question as to whether the population of the GDR should really be given the opportunity of determining their fate "by making a free choice". He too demanded of the GDR that it should grant its population the fundamental human rights. And this should apply with equal force to the social institutions of eastern Germany: the right to independent trade unions for the workers; the right of the farming population to cultivate the land on their own responsibility and to decide freely on the forms of production; the right of craftsmen to operate independent businesses; the right of writers and artists to creative activity outside the control of the party and the state; and for the sciences the right to research and teach in their own way. But all this amounted to nothing less than a coming together of the two parts of Germany, and bilateral recognition, the ultimate aim of which would be that one day the GDR would cease to be *the* German Democratic Republic.

So far as its official attitude was concerned, the grand coalition continued to maintain the view that the GDR population should be given the opportunity of expressing themselves openly and freely determining their own future. Chancellor Kiesinger reiterated this policy in an interview with the *Stuttgarter Nachrichten* on 28 February 1967, in which he sought at the same time to deny any intention of "annexing" the GDR. When it was put to the Chancellor that this silent area of Germany was a blank spot on the European map, he replied that the other part of Germany existed whether or not Ulbricht was recognised.

Our only objective is to help to pave the way for political expression by the population in the other half of Germany.... Up until the present time, the people who live there have beeen denied the opportunity of freely expressing their opinions on the shape of peacetime Europe, the solution of the German national question, or even the pattern of their own lives. This is why we cannot recognise those who wish to maintain the present situation.

This went beyond the idea of allowing one part of Germany a voice in what went on in the other part, and was in effect a hangover of the reunification policy which both Germanies had in their constitutions as a binding obligation. But the Germany towards which each of the two Germanies aspired was one to be cast in their own respective image. Even the idea of working together, and each having a say in the other's affairs, meant that a united Germany would only be possible if one of the German states changed its ways: if the Federal Republic renounced capitalism or the GDR gave up dictatorship.

It soon became evident that the GDR not only demanded recognition, but also recognition with no strings attached. For a long time the Federal Republic refused to credit the fact that the GDR really meant what it said and so made the old mistake of not taking the other side seriously, of doubting whether its words corresponded to its views, and of making demands which directly conflicted with their much repeated position. The attitude of the Soviet Union and the GDR was fixed, however dubious the basic premisses might be: namely, that the GDR had a right to recognition under international law: and that its existence as an independent state with all the characteristics of sovereignty is an indisputable fact. Therefore the recognition of the GDR cannot be made conditional upon a treaty negotiated on a quid pro quo basis. There should be no talk of concessions when recognising something to which the owners have an indisputable right and of which they are in complete and inviolable possession.

The GDR, in the words of the SED authorities, scarcely needs to be recognised anyway; but the Federal Republic has to recognise the realities of the European situation—the GDR, the Oder-Neisse line, among other things—if it is to extricate itself from the dangerous position in which it finds itself, and to cease standing in the way of international progress. Otherwise the Federal Republic would be denying the inexorable judgement passed on the Third Reich by the Second World War. It appeared, argued the SED, that the Federal Republic did not wish to accept the fact that the Hitler Reich had been smashed once and for all by the defeat which it had brought upon itself, and thus the Federal Republic was seriously risking unleashing a second disaster. Only recognition of the realities of the situation—and in particular of the GDR—would point the way for the Federal Republic out of this fruitless and suicidal resistance to the inevitable onward march of events.

All these problems were thrown up when the question of recognition began to be discussed in earnest. Up until that time recognition of the GDR was regarded simply as treasonable. Under the governments of Adenauer and Erhard no one would have ventured to prophesy that recognition would cease to be a taboo subject within a few years and would moreover become an important part of government policy. But for a while the hope still remained of transforming the GDR into a free and democratic country, either as a precondition for or as a result of recognition. If they showed nothing else, the opening rounds in the fight over recognition demonstrated that the GDR was not interested in conditions or mutual concessions. But it demanded courage to have got this far without having made any gains, at least no visible gains. The statesman who does such a thing must risk coming home empty-handed, or at the least without seeming to have made any gains—in the same way that Konrad Adenauer in Moscow in 1955 boldly signed the mutual recognition pact between the Federal Republic and the USSR without having achieved any more than a verbal promise about what the Russians were doing in return; that is, releasing the prisoners-of-war.

Recognition would mean taking the courageous step of giving credence to concessions which would only be made by word of mouth, and which could be broken at any time, and having faith in the hope that recognition would conspire with the weight of events to improve the quality of life.

It is only natural to ask why the Oder-Neisse line or the independent existence of the GDR—which no power on earth would seem likely to be able to remove in the foreseeable future—needed recognition so badly. It is indeed remarkable how much weight the Soviet authorities and their subordinates place upon official and legal recognition. It is all too easy to turn up quotations from the leaders of the Bolshevists, according to which treaties—these "scraps of paper"—have about as much teeth to them as a paper tiger—for behind the smokescreen of non-aggression and friendship treaties the relentless struggle rages on. But the states of eastern Europe did not take kindly to the fact that important elements of their political systems were regarded by the west as illegal and they themselves as renegades. This was the root cause of the enmity between east and west. And the enmity itself has been an important factor in the extreme efforts by the populations of the eastern bloc countries which have made the substantial sacrifices demanded of them in building up industrialised societies. But all observers agree that economic advancement, particularly in the Soviet Union, had reached a point at which it became evident that closer contact with technical progress in the west was a matter of urgency. The agreements with the Federal Republic could be regarded as an expression of willingness on the part of the Soviet Union to move some way away from complete isolation from the west.

In all the diplomatic statements and in all the treaties the cause and basis for this change of heart is given as the "return to normality." Of course, a social order which has torn its people apart and erects walls at national frontiers is not to be considered normal. But the absence of any kind of relations between one state and another is in itself abnormal; and it is abnormal for nations not to live in peace with one another. For peace is neither love nor friendship; it is a state of international give and take, the sum total of those international rules of conduct which also hold good for enemies and men whose ways of life are worlds apart. In classical times, the absence of diplomatic relations was synonymous with a state of war; and breaking off diplomatic relations was often another way of declaring war: "Inter pacem et bellum nullum tertium est." (There is no intermediary stage between peace and war.)

Even Kiesinger's government wanted to bring an end to the absence of diplomatic relations with eastern Europe, because it meant that otherwise west Germany's frontiers to the east would be bordering on a void. It was and remains unnatural to treat the territories between the Federal Republic and the Soviet Union as if they did not exist, for these nations had for centuries had the closest ties with Germany. Nature abhors a vacuum. And the areas to the east of the iron curtain certainly represented a political vacuum. But it is impossible to disregard the facts of a given situation. Non-recognition did make sense for as long as there were reasonable grounds to doubt the durability of the eastern states in the form they had taken, and for as long as the hope remained that non-recognition would have a real effect and frighten the non-recognised states out of existence.

On 31 January 1967 Jugoslavia and the Federal Republic re-established diplomatic relations which had been broken off after Jugoslavia had recognised the GDR. On the same day the Federal Republic and Rumania formally completed mutual recognition and a treaty on the establishment of embassies was signed. This marked a break with the Hallstein doctrine, the principle enunciated by a professor which states that no country could have diplomatic relations with the two Germanies simultaneously; and this principle had already forfeited some of its persuasiveness in 1955 when the

Soviet Union forced the Federal Republic into taking up diplomatic relations.

Even after the Federal Republic had set up embassies in Bucharest and Belgrade, it continued to look unfavourably on all those states—especially the emergent nations of Africa and America—which simultaneously took up diplomatic relations with the GDR. The authority of the Federal Republic and its financial strength were for a long time strong enough to frighten many states away from entering into diplomatic relations with the GDR, and thereby indulging in a relationship which in the eyes of international law was a kind of bigamy. But at times it became a little too expensive for the Federal Republic to pay out to these new nations in hard cash. And other nations argued that the Federal Republic was not setting a very good example itself. "Where the judge steals, the thief too has a right to steal." It sounded like the death-rattle of a moribund hypothesis when the Federal Republic again aired its claim to sole recognition when setting up relations with Rumania. The Foreign Office stated in a verbal note on 31 January to all accredited embassies and legations that "taking up diplomatic relations with Rumania did not signify any change in the view of the law taken by the Federal government—and repeated in the government statement of 13 December 1966—that, as the freely, legally and democratically elected German government it has the right to speak for the entire German nation."

According to this note, it was the aim of the Federal Republic to enter into diplomatic relations with other eastern neighbours. The accompanying reduction in tension would however be prejudiced if the nations with which the Federal Republic had diplomatic relations were to draw erroneous conclusions from this policy. This was as good as saying that the Federal Republic would continue to regard the recognition of the GDR by states with whom it had diplomatic relations as an unfriendly act. The policy on which this verbal note was based could be stated in these terms : there is a fundamental distinction to be drawn between efforts on the part of the Federal Republic directed towards diplomatic representation with countries where "Germany" is already inadequately represented by the GDR, and the acceptance of diplomatic missions by countries where the Federal Republic is already represented, unless there are compelling special circumstances. The reaction of the Soviet Union could hardly have been sharper and more disapproving than in the reply to the Bonn note : the Russians claimed that the Federal government's statement flew in the face of the facts of the European situation and all international agreements which state "that the Federal government only exercises power within its own territorial boundaries." It is foolish in the extreme for the Federal government to claim that it alone has the duty and obligation of speaking for the entire German nation. For this reason the Soviet government gave the embassy of the USSR in Bonn instructions to return the note on account of the blatant unacceptability of its contents. The Soviet Union presented a catalogue of demands on its own account in respect of German policy in the east, and the Federal Republic found itself confronted with these demands right up to the Moscow negotiations of 1970. These were to the effect that the Federal government should take account of the real state of affairs in Europe, that is, it should work on the basis of the existence of two German states, which means that there should be no more insistence on reshaping European frontiers nor on the claim to be the sole representative of Germany. Equally it should desist from putting pressure on those states prepared to recognise the GDR. Finally, the Soviet note declared that the Federal government was not measuring up to its obligations under the Potsdam agreement, because Nazi organisations were being allowed to exist and no attempt was being made to inhibit the resurgence of Nazi ideology. In subsequent notes the Soviet Union had pointed out in a threatening note that Articles 53 and 107 of the UN Charter gave it the right to take action against a former enemy state if in its estimation that state constituted a threat of war.

The right of the victorious powers to intervene is contained in nearly all treaties relating to Germany since the Second World War. The shape of the two Germanies on either side of the iron curtain now can be traced directly back to the unlimited right of the victors, and this is the basis upon which all the Allies took their first measures in Germany.

But the unilateral intervention of one of the victorious powers in one part of Germany which is still under occupation by another power is perilously close to the eventuality of war foreseen in the NATO and Warsaw Pact treaties.

Threat and inducement rubbed shoulders; the attitudes of the Warsaw Pact countries were similar, for they were prepared to enter into a treaty agreement with the Federal Republic (a few short years ago this would have been regarded as treacherous pact-mongering with capitalism and Nazism), as long as it did not offend against the frontiers established in 1945 and met the approval of neighbouring states. A conference of the Eastern bloc countries in February 1967 expressed its strongest disapproval of the Federal Republic's claim to be the sole true representative of Germany. Solidarity with the GDR, a country which for them acted as a buffer against the Federal Republic, remained by and large unbroken. "I do not know," the First Secretary of the central committee of the Hungarian Communist Party, Kadar, exclaimed, "what you would say if Ulbricht's comrades were to maintain that they alone had a legal basis for their existence and that from now on they were going to represent the entire German nation. I declare here and now that they have the greater right to do so, for they represent the future of the German nation." Then, he continued, a fresh start could be made. What Kadar meant by "a fresh start" was a return to a situation in Germany in which each of the two states sought the dissolution of the other and each gave itself out as the sole true Germany. In the east, a divided Germany seemed to be less dangerous than a united Germany, even one under Communist rule.

The People's Republic of Hungary, declared Kadar, sought "to pave the way towards normal diplomatic, economic and cultural relationships with all countries prepared to accept them." And in the situation of February 1967 this could only be a reference to the Federal Republic.

Although the party leadership of the FDP had its reservations, it did not condemn out of hand the very wide range of proposals for putting the German situation on a proper basis; such proposals were fully in accordance with the logic of events, but they were put forward without the trepidation that must have been felt when the old Germany was divided into two under the surgeon's knife. On the surface, the policies of the Federal government in 1970 are in some respects close to these proposals; but they have been put into practice in a different spirit and on the basis of different political attitudes. Those who drew up all those plans for Germany, as practical politicians in a situation of helplessness and surrender, were in the main content to write off the idea of a German nation and a united Germany without any great emotional upheaval. In contrast, Brandt's government is striving passionately to keep alive the awareness of a united Germany as a practical proposition, and regards its policy not as the end of the struggle for Germany, but as a new beginning and a new initiative.

But in the meantime more and more voices in the Federal Republic have been raised in favour of relinquishing such aspirations. In their view the Germans are not suited for unification. The national state, in the form that Bismarck created it, was a tragic adventure doomed to end in bloody defeat. Reunification seemed not only impossible, but also undesirable and a threat to Europe.

So for all the similarity between the practical propositions of the FDP and the Federal government's actions in 1970, the spirit and attitudes are different. What the proposals sought was to put an end to that insane notion called Germany. The government, on the other hand, seeks to find a new point of departure for the re-establishment of German national unity.

The chief press officer of the FDP, Wolfgang Scholwer, put forward a working document in March 1967 in which he analysed the current position of Germany:

> On German territory two German states have now grown up. It must be admitted that the GDR was not founded on the basis of free democratic elections, but in practice it performs all the functions which a state normally takes upon itself; and the dissolution of the GDR cannot be effected either by force or negotiation. The GDR has long since become part of a post-war European order which is broadly speaking in a state of balance, and its continuing existence is not in the interest of the east alone; the reunification of Germany, under whatever conditions it took place, would lead to a total disruption of the balance of power in Europe, let alone the fact that all European nations have a profound fear of a German national state with 75 million inhabitants and the strongest economy on the continent and are doing their utmost to prevent it.

That is tantamount to an obituary.

In March of the same year the party treasurer of the FDP, Hans-Wolfgang Rubin, published a study of the German problem under the title *Die Stunde der Wahrheit* (The Hour of Truth).

> The truth, however unpalatable it may be, must not be expressed just by the few, but by those in positions of responsibility, and the majority of the people must understand and accept it: and the truth of the matter is that Germany was responsible for the Second World War, lost it utterly and subsequently accepted unconditional surrender. The truth of the matter is that friend and foe alike are agreed that it is neither possible nor desirable to reconstitute the German Reich within its 1937 frontiers.

This hour of truth is truly a time for an exhausted and broken nation to despair.

There is, however, no foundation in Rubin's argument that reunification is synonymous with the reinstatement of the 1937 boundaries, for in fact the establishment of an all-German state could be considered within the context of any number of different boundary lines. No one in his right mind could believe that it would be possible to resurrect the Germany of 1937 from the grave where Hitler's Reich met its terrible end. It is foolish indeed to cherish the notion that the Reich could still continue to exist with all the territory in its former possession after the horror and its grisly defeat. Germany cannot put the clock back.

Brandt once said that what disturbed him above all about the word reunification was the prefix "re-" which implied a return of things as they had been before.

But it is equally foolish to set 1945 as the crucial moment in

German history. Neither of these dates, 1937 or 1945, should be regarded as fixed and immovable. For any nation defeat always constitutes a "moment of unreality," because a true and lasting relationship between nations should not be determined when one side is looking down from the dizzy heights of victory. In the hour of military defeat the victor is all and the defeated nothing, but this should never be allowed to form the basis of a lasting relationship between them. There is virtually no hope of success in an attempt to keep one of the great nations in a state of impotence for any length of time. But on the other side of the coin, there is equally little hope of sweeping aside the memory of defeat just as if it were a bad dream.

The GDR also appeared to be acting responsibly in rejecting the notions of "Germany" and "German." It is true that those in power kept on stressing that it was the capitalists and Fascists of the Federal Republic who had killed "Germany." As a consequence the name of Germany had become a laughing-stock. This was why the name of the "State secretariat for all-German questions" was altered to "State secretariat for West German questions," and for this reason too the regulation was issued that the Social Democratic party of Germany should henceforth be known simply as the Social Democratic party. "Our responsibilities as a nation demand that it should be made clear beyond all possible doubt that in the present situation, as a result of the guilt of west German monopoly capitalism and its Bonn régime together with its Social Democratic ministers, terms like 'all-German' have become utterly meaningless."

The "law relating to citizenship of the GDR" does away with the notion of "German citizenship" and denies its own constitution which had stated that "there is only one form of German citizenship." This is contradicted by the statement in the 1967 law to the effect that "with the foundation of the GDR came, in accordance with international law, citizenship of the GDR. This is an expression of the sovereignty of the GDR." Secretary of State Ritter von Hase replied on behalf of the Federal government with some feeling : "The Federal government by contrast declares in full accordance with the will of the German people as a whole that there are not two nations, there is only one German people." And now the question was whether the German people could measure up to the greatest burden that could be imposed upon a nation, namely, that of remaining a nation once the protective skin of a unified state had been broken.

The GDR did not tire of seeking recognition under international law and of proposing a meeting between the heads of government of the two German states which would serve the purpose of finalising this recognition. A speech by the chairman of the GDR state council at the beginning of 1967 expounded this declaration which has up to the present moment been pursued unflinchingly by those in power in the GDR and gives a strong sense of direction to GDR policy.

Despite the usual posturing and stereotyped attacks on the "revanchist and imperialist Federal Republic," the fact that both German states had an independent historical existence was clearly recognised and expressed in no uncertain terms. Ulbricht's proposals naturally reveal the specific goals which he and the GDR were pursuing. But they still gave the impetus for the first negotiations, which took place between the two German states in 1970 after lengthy diplomatic activity.

Ulbricht's forceful stand against those who regarded a working relationship between the two German states as impossible is particularly striking, as is his explicit declaration in favour of German unity. What should not be forgotten is that at that time Ulbricht described the negotiations between the two German states as a "link" between them, that the ominous formula "recognition under international law" does not yet appear and that all that is mentioned is "the establishment of normal relations." What Ulbricht outlined in his speech was formulated in a letter which the Prime Minister of the GDR, Willi Stoph, sent to the Federal Chancellor on 10 May 1967. Stoph refers to Ulbricht's declarations. He broadly repeats the proposals put forward by Ulbricht, namely, that the Federal Republic must recognise the realities of the situation—this is a phrase that keeps cropping up—and above all else surrender the claim to being the sole true representative of Germany, a claim which is both illegal and a threat to peace. There is even a touch of black humour : the Federal Republic declares emphatically that it seeks to "loosen up" relations between the two states. The best way of doing that, the letter states, would surely be for the Federal Republic to pay its debts to the GDR.

The Federal Chancellor replied on 13 June to the effect that the letter from the GDR Prime Minister was based on the well-known "all or nothing" principle. Instead of helping the situation by practical measures, his sole intention was to maintain the split.

Nor did the Federal Chancellor shrink back from telling the GDR Prime Minister to his face that his régime was not truly representative of the people of the GDR.

> As long as these people are denied the opportunity of expressing their will in regard to the fate of their nation without fear or favour, the freely elected government of the Federal Republic bears the responsibility for acting as their spokesman as well.

It was a perfectly reasonable attitude to maintain that the régime of the GDR did not represent the people. In all the conversations and negotiations with the GDR there arose the serious and undeniable objection that no one knows and no one can know whether or to what extent negotiations and agreements meet with the approbation of the German people in the GDR. All negotiations would have to rest on the highly suspect hypothesis that the population of the GDR shared the convictions of their government in seeking to turn the GDR into a fully independent sovereign state. It has been justifiably pointed out that the preconditions for "statehood" which are normally imposed are satisfied in the case of the GDR : state territory, state population, power in the hands of the state. No one doubts that the GDR government is in a position to maintain stability and order within its territories, and these are the usual conditions laid down for "recognition." But—and this is the nub of the matter—recognition of the GDR would bring in its train recognition of the fact that it exists as an entity which has separated itself from a longstanding political and national unit. In cases where states have split off from a larger structure, other powers—when confronting the question of recognition—do not simply operate the tests of territory, population and authority, but also whether it is possible to approve the destruction of the old state and the existence of the smaller national units.

It is more than reasonable to doubt whether the GDR can permit freedom in its state without imperilling its own existence; and it is also more than reasonable to refrain from negotiations with a régime which denies its citizens the freedom to express their opinions and which can therefore never represent the will of the people. But the consequence of such an attitude is that one would have to wait until such a régime ceased to exist. Until then—and that time may never come—there would not be the least possibility of entering into meaningful negotiations with the other half of Germany. The solution of the German question becomes impossible under such circumstances, unless it be through the destruction of the régime in the other half of Germany either by military force or revolution.

But it has turned out to be the case that such hanging about and waiting, living with the "great impossibility," imposes excessive demands on the resources of the German people.

It was a long and wearisome business establishing relations with eastern Europe. Up until 1970 diplomatic relations had only been established with Rumania and Yugoslavia.

The Federal Republic concluded a trade agreement with Czechoslovakia on 1 August 1967. The Federal German negotiators were unable to get more than an agreement and the establishment of trade missions; the Czechs sidestepped discussions of relations on a diplomatic and political level. Still, there is not a complete absence of relations between states which have mutual trade agreements. The Czechs were quite content with a trade pact with its positive advantages for themselves, and in exchange they only had to tolerate a symbolic presence of the Federal Republic on their territory in the shape of the trade mission.

After a longish interval the dialogue between the Federal Republic and the GDR was resumed once more. On 18 September 1967 the Prime Minister of the GDR gave his reply to the correspondence from Federal Chancellor Kiesinger dated 10 May. The battle of words had been held in suspense throughout the summer, but it was no more than an interlude. Tempers had hardly cooled. Stoph's answer was aggressive and polemical in the extreme. His anger at the Federal Republic's claim to being the sole representative of the German people was understandable, to say the least. No government likes to have it said of itself that it is not empowered to speak on behalf of its own population. "The organs of the state elected by the people are alone able to act and speak on behalf of the population." In trying to deny the realities of the situation and in seeking to sweep them under the carpet, the Federal Republic was really aspiring towards a retrospective victory in the war. This time Stoph also stated quite openly that the GDR were equally interested in detaching the Federal Republic from its western influence. So the main stumbling block in the way of agreement between the two Germanies was western Germany's treaty obligations. The entry of the Federal Republic into the EEC was "diametrically opposed to the process of unification."

Stoph attached to his letter a "draft treaty"; this is what he called the appended catalogue of requests and demands directed at the Federal Republic. It contained points which could not possibly be settled in a treaty between the GDR and the Federal Republic (for example, recognition by the Federal Republic that the Munich agreement was null and void from the start). Other points concern matters which could not be formulated in a legal framework or within the context of a treaty or which were not so worded in Stoph's catalogue.

None the less the East Berlin régime spelled out clearly for the very first time what they meant by "normal relations" between the GDR and the Federal Republic. In relations between the two countries "the generally recognised principles of international law are a fundamental consideration."

These relations should take on the form of those "between sovereign states of the German nation striving towards peaceful coexistence and a gradual process of rapprochement."

The catalogue of so-called basic principles which the two states were supposed to observe includes non-intervention in the internal affairs of other states, recognition of the existing frontiers inclusive of the Oder-Neisse line and the frontier between the GDR and the Federal Republic, recognition that the Munich agreement is invalid, and also renunciation of the use of atomic weapons. The two states were to undertake to institute negotiations with the objective of "the peaceful solution of national questions," normalising relationships between the two, carrying out a common disarmament policy, concluding an agreement on European security, and "on the basis of overcoming militarism, Neo-Nazism and the power of monopoly capitalism."

It was the same on both sides : the Federal Republic only wanted to begin formal talks with the GDR when its people were allowed to express their views freely, and the GDR only wanted to discuss national issues with the Federal Republic when "the power of monopoly capitalism" was broken there. Neither of the two Germanies seemed prepared to start talking to the other until it had changed radically and surrendered its own basic principles of existence.

The reply of the Federal Chancellor dated 29 September 1967 to the letter from the Prime Minister of the GDR is directed entirely at the notion of self-determination for the German people with the objective of reunification. It is to the German people as a whole, who alone really have the right to choose, and before whom the GDR has to justify itself, that the appeal is really being made. In this spirit the Federal Chancellor insisted that the contents of his letter should not be withheld from the population in the east of Germany.

> It is our conviction that the German nation, whose existence you too recognise, is politically adult and should be allowed to form its own judgement on the issues before it. Polemics will get nowhere. The German people are the real rulers and it is our conviction that they wish to live together in a single state. The will of the nation determines our own actions. Among the peoples of the world the right of self-determination is not disputed. The day will come when this right will no longer be able to be denied to the German people. It is the duty of all Germans to pave the way towards this solution of the German question by just and peaceful means.

The Federal government declared its readiness to enter into negotiations on this matter. The Secretary of State of the Federal Republic would hold himself in permanent readiness for this purpose.

## EXCHANGE OF NOTES WITH THE SOVIET UNION: IS A NON-AGGRESSION PACT ON THE CARDS?

Would it be possible for the Federal Republic to be able to negotiate with the Soviet Union over the head of the GDR? It all depended on finding out whether the Soviet Union stood firmly behind the demands of the GDR. It did not appear very likely that the GDR would put forward demands of this order without being certain of Soviet backing, but it was worth having a go at bilateral non-aggression treaties with individual countries in the eastern bloc, starting with the Soviet Union.

However, it soon became evident that the Soviet Union was determined to bring all the treaties the Federal Republic concluded with eastern bloc countries under one heading and to turn them into a single unified treaty document. The Russians wanted to conduct these negotiations on the basis of their supreme power and leadership in the eastern bloc. In this spirit they laid down in their notes to the Federal Republic how the Germans should come to terms with Poland, Czechoslovakia and the GDR. Not unnaturally, the Federal Republic sought to treat negotiations with the GDR as a separate issue unconnected with the question of general recognition of the eastern bloc states. Statements from the Federal government made it clear that non-aggression was a special matter in relation to the GDR, because the GDR was still continuing to exert force and was itself founded on force. But there was not much prospect of success in an attempt to separate out the GDR. The Federal government, the Federal Chancellor and the Foreign Minister all took the view that it was at the least too early, if not impossible altogether, to discuss the fundamental principles of relations between the GDR and the Federal Republic. They sought limited agreements with the immediate objective of achieving a modicum of peaceful coexistence between the two states and of sparing the German population the sufferings caused by the enmity between the two states. Any negotiations with the GDR on non-aggression could not help but touch upon the basic elements of the relations between the two states. Non-aggression agreements are included in all treaties between independent states; and what is meant by "aggression" is usually war. This is the reason why the Federal government did not want to enter into negotiations with the GDR on this issue, for they would of necessity "upvalue" the GDR to the level of a state.

But the Federal government cleverly concealed the fact that it did not want to deal with the GDR on the question of non-aggression in its solemn declaration that its promise not to resort to force also applied without reservation to the other half of Germany.

However, the Federal government did not pull it off. It was asked with increasing urgency and in the end quite bluntly if it intended to conduct the same negotiations and conclude the same kind of treaty with the GDR as with the other eastern bloc countries. If this was the case, then the Federal government would finally have to accept the offer of treating with the GDR as well on the subject of a non-aggression pact. And the German public saw this happen in the "Report of the Federal government on the nation in a divided Germany" dated 11 March 1968. Up to this point the Federal government had gone no further than to propose negotiations on "all practical issues relating to German coexistence." But now the Federal Chancellor added the following : "The Federal government henceforth expressly broadens the proposed topics for negotiation to include the issue of non-aggression." "Henceforth" meant that from that moment on—but not before—the Federal government was prepared to deal directly with the GDR on the question of non-aggression.

But in order to set events clearly in their context we have slipped out of chronological sequence. Let us look back now to see how this state of affairs came about. The Federal government had been negotiating secretly with Ambassador Zarapkin who had clearly failed to explain in sufficient detail what precisely the Soviet Union wanted the package deal to contain, namely non-aggression.

In any event, the Federal government was somewhat offended when the Soviet government made it clear in a statement handed over by Ambassador Zarapkin on 12 October 1967 that the Russians sought nothing less than a non-aggression pact between the Federal Republic and the GDR : "The frontier between the Federal Republic and the GDR is in reality the sole frontier where a direct threat of aggression is likely to occur." If the Federal government were to refuse to conduct direct negotiations with the GDR this would indicate that its objectives with respect to the GDR were following a course irreconcilable with the notion of non-aggression. And the claim to be the sole representative of the German people flew in the face of the facts. "The sovereign rights and interests of the GDR must be recognised unconditionally and illegal incursions in Berlin must cease." (By this is meant the economic and political links between West Berlin and the Federal Republic.)

The crucial point in the Soviet note is contained in the statement that the Russians would only be prepared to sign a non-aggression pact with the Federal Republic if the latter declared its own readiness to exchange similar agreements with the GDR.

The Soviet government also took the view that any links between West Berlin and the Federal Republic were "revisionist" and an affront to the outcome of the Second World War because they posed a threat to the GDR's claim to absolute sovereignty over the entire city.

It also appeared to the Russians that the Federal Republic was also cherishing secret "revisionist" desires in its refusal to recognise that the Munich agreement "and everything consequent upon it" was null and void. The Munich agreement "was part of a criminal conspiracy on the part of Nazi Germany"; and the Russians all too clearly suspected that everyone who did not dismiss the Munich agreement out of hand sought to continue the conspiracy. The Soviet note went even further: if the Federal Republic did not renounce the use of force (in the manner which had just been prescribed) then the Warsaw Pact countries would have to take the appropriate measures on their own responsibility. Never again should the threat of war be allowed to grow up on German soil. In the Potsdam agreement the Allied states had been united in their resolve to seek to prevent this eventuality by all possible means. And, as one of the legal successors to the Nazi Reich, the Federal Republic was bound to the Potsdam agreement which had "the validity of an international obligation."

Until such time as a peace treaty had been concluded, the Soviet government indicated that it reserved the right to take steps against any danger that might arise from within the Federal Republic.

In all the Soviet notes the Federal Republic's refusal to relinquish Berlin was a bone of contention. In the eyes of the Russians Berlin was clear evidence of the erosion of what they regarded as a secure prize of war. What was evidently behind the Russian dealings on the non-aggression issue was the firm resolve not to let the same thing happen again. In the first stages of the non-aggression negotiations it seemed that the Russian objective was separation of West Berlin from the Federal Republic. Anyone seeking to make West Berlin a dependency of the Federal Republic was in effect challenging Russian victory in war—this was how the Russian notes expressed it more or less directly. The very existence of West Berlin in its present form was a provocation, "an act of aggression," as the Soviet leaders maintained on many occasions.

But on the issue of Berlin the Soviet government met with the stiffest and most determined resistance. Soon an opposing trend began to make itself felt towards making the planned agreements dependent upon guarantees for West Berlin and its increased security. There is of course a fundamental distinction to be drawn between concessions in non-aggression pacts with the eastern bloc countries and surrender on the part of the west in respect of Berlin. The "abandonment" of the territories beyond the Oder-Neisse line, of the GDR or the Sudetenland is something which would only happen on paper and have no more than a legalistic and ideological significance. After all, the Federal Republic did not possess any of these territories any more. Berlin, on the other hand, was still a tangible possession that would actually have to be given away and yielded up.

More and more the new Ostpolitik came to hinge upon Berlin. At times it gave the negotiations on non-aggression an unreal quality because they were on a totally different plane from the Berlin negotiations, but the Federal Republic had declared that the one depended on the other. In reality each of the non-aggression pacts raised the Berlin question from a different point of view. For non-aggression and the position of Berlin in the European and German context had always been mutually dependent issues which cannot be considered in isolation one from the other. The Germans must have known when they were in Moscow in 1970 what kind of accommodation on Berlin was to be expected. The Soviet Foreign Minister behaved like a schizophrenic: the Gromyko who was negotiating with the Germans in Moscow seemed not to have anything to do with the other Gromyko under whose instructions the Soviet representatives at the four-power conference were discussing Berlin. It was Moscow's intention that Berlin and treaties with the Federal Republic in relation to its position in the system of east European states should be dealt with separately.

In reply to the opinions voiced in favour of giving in among the German public at large an association called Germany Undivided was formed in 1954; its declarations and communiqués had a largely semi-official character and often served as feelers to discover how Germany and the world at large reacted to specific situations and propositions. In January 1968 the executive chairman of the association, Wilhelm Wolfgang Schütz, proposed that the Federal Republic's claim to sole representation of the German people should be surrendered:

> Have the Federal government and parliament effectively been representing the people living outside the territories in which the Federal constitution operates? It is impossible to answer this with an unequivocal affirmative.... There has never really been any question of proper representation. In practical terms it has been impossible.

Schütz argued that the population of the GDR were no longer absolutely opposed to their state and were passively waiting for some power to take up their cause. "Using their own resources and in the absence of peaceful alternatives they have come to terms with life in the GDR. . . . It is impossible for them to avoid identifying themselves with the GDR in everyday life. That does not necessarily mean that in their hearts they identify with the system and its ideology, nor with the lack of freedom."

It was well-nigh self-evident that the association Germany Undivided regarded the division of Germany as an impossibility: "The debate on the issue of recognition or non-recognition of the two German states makes no sense at all. Recognition or non-recognition is something that happens between states that are quite separate. In the context of Germany the issue is meaningless."

Schütz equally considered it a waste of time to discuss whether mutually incompatible social systems can coexist within a single state fabric, for the fact of the matter was that they were indeed living side by side.

The GDR on the other hand maintained the view that the incompatibility of the social and political systems in the two Germanies rendered the emergence of a common state impossible. But it was not impossible for the two states to be regarded as separate under international law. Sovereignty was not an ethical issue, but a matter of practical politics.

The public debate was a reflection of the dialogue between the governments. The Soviet Union and the Federal Republic were engaged in an exchange of notes that varied considerably in tone and cordiality.

As has already been indicated, the Soviet Union had its sights firmly fixed upon concrete attainable objectives, namely, securing in full the conquests of victory, even if the Soviet Union had to refer right back to the right of the victor and the Potsdam resolutions, which were founded solely on unconditional surrender, in order to do so. All this sounds like a resolve to sweep away the ruins that still remained from the old Germany which was smashed in 1945. Non-aggression by itself had no real significance for the Russians; in their treaty drafts it was a mere hollow affirmation. The Soviet notes made it all too clear that they regarded as "a threat to its power" any attempt to break down the frontiers and the states which had emerged as an outcome of the war. One of the Soviet notes went as far as to state that non-recognition of the results of the World War was tantamount to plotting a new World War. A solemn declaration of non-aggression must be preceded by the firm resolve to master the present situation in the most concrete manner possible.

The resolution of the questions that remain unsettled between the Federal Republic on the one hand and Poland, Czechoslovakia and the GDR on the other should not be regarded as a result and a conclusion to negotiations on non-aggression, but their beginning, their starting-point, a proof of the actuality and reality of non-aggression. In its note of 9 April 1968 the Federal government took a quite different view. The west Germans were concerned to give precedence to general principles and to make non-aggression—which should form the basis for a new international order—a separate issue in its own right, rather than allow it to become lost in a maze of individual questions. They stated that the Russians were seeking to resolve all manner of issues at the same time as coming to an agreement on non-aggression. What the Federal government was proposing on the other hand was to take things a step at a time, since individual questions can be extremely complicated. The best starting-point would be an agreement on non-use of force or the threat of force, and this would create a better climate for negotiations on individual and specific problems.

The west German note specifically accepted the Russian view that a non-aggression pact with the Soviet Union would only be meaningful if a similar exchange of declarations was also undertaken with Poland and Czechoslovakia. The Federal government also recognised the fact that the Poles and Czechs were concerned, not with principles, but with resolving specific points of issue between themselves and the Federal government. In its declaration of readiness "also to discuss a non-aggression pact with the other part of Germany" the note lets drop a discreet hint that discussions with the GDR would represent a special case : the Federal government, the note states, saw in discussions with the GDR on the question of non-aggression a step in the direction of reducing tension and a "rapprochement between the two parts of Germany, which do not regard each other as foreign powers." The Federal note also brings a shift of emphasis in relation to the Munich agreement. The one sentence which refers to this matter starts off in one way and ends up quite differently : the Federal government took the view that "an agreement which was brought about under threat of force could no longer be valid," but insofar as this related to the invalidity of the Munich agreement in that it came about under threat of force, then it was invalid from the outset, and the words "no longer valid" were not a logical consequence of the first part of the sentence.

The attitude to the Potsdam agreement was an unfair reply to an unfair attempt to lay a trap for the Federal Republic on the basis of the Potsdam statements. The basis of the Potsdam edicts on the treatment of Germany was unconditional surrender and bears the stamp of the immediate post-war years in which Germany was not allowed any will of its own.

By refusing to adopt an attitude in respect to the Potsdam agreement, the Federal Republic was mischievously making its position very clear. "With regard to the repeatedly expressed views of the Soviet government on the meaning of the Potsdam agreement of 1945, it is the view of the Federal Republic that it is not within its competence to express itself on the interpretation and validity of agreements to which it has not been party."

The Federal note concluded by stating that it also seemed inappropriate in discussions on non-aggression for the Soviet government to adduce from the Potsdam agreement and the UN Charter the right of intervention by force.

> If the government of the USSR were united with the Federal Republic in the desire to exclude the application of force or the threat of force from their mutual relations, then it would be contrary to the sense and objectives of such an agreement for the Soviet government to cite the UN Charter and reserve the right to use force against any peaceful European states, including the Federal Republic.

In the negotiations the Federal Republic presupposes an acceptance of the basic principles of sovereignty and non-intervention. That sentence is also an unambiguous reference to Potsdam and the right of intervention. The reply from the Soviet government was one of calculated rudeness:

> It is recorded with regret that in the memorandum of 9 April from the Federal government there is not one single sentence that gives evidence of any real effort to demonstrate a constructive and relevant approach to the Soviet proposals which had been communicated to the West Germans. The reply of the Federal government makes it perfectly clear it would like to proceed with an exchange of declarations on non-aggression with the Soviet Union and the other socialist countries in such a way that its whole revanchist attitude in all the principal issues of European security remains unshaken.

In reply to the Federal government's innocent declaration to the effect that the Potsdam agreement was none of its concern, the Soviet government lavished praise upon this unwonted accord. "The enduring significance of the principles of the Potsdam agreement has been confirmed by the whole course of events since the war in Europe and the world at large, and the Soviet Union, which along with other east European countries stands in the forefront of the struggle for peace, considers it a solemn obligation to protect and defend these principles."

All previous Russian notes sounded as if the judgement of Potsdam were now finally to be made.

The negotiations were deadlocked. On 20 June Foreign Minister Brandt summarised the situation: the basic position of Soviet policy with regard to Germany as a whole had hardly shifted at all.

Then came the occupation of Czechoslovakia by Soviet troops. The world once more saw with its own eyes that the Soviet Union was incorrigible, that it would always remain a power-hungry Communist state, sworn to world revolution. It soon became evident that the Soviet army did not intend to march on and sweep across Europe, but the impression remained that the action taken by the Russians was directed against self-determination by all nations, and that those tanks rolling pitilessly onward were an expression of Russian scorn for the peaceful aspirations of all nations. It seemed pointless to go any further with negotiations with the Soviet Union based on non-intervention in the internal affairs of a country and on non-aggression.

It seemed too far-fetched to subscribe to the notion that the action against Czechoslovakia and the non-aggression pact could possibly be both working in one and the same direction, namely the consolidation of the Soviet empire.

Any further developments towards settling the question of Germany seemed incomprehensible to those who idealised the idea of a non-aggression pact and who regarded events like the occupation of Czechoslovakia as a lapse on the part of a Soviet Union which was treading the path toward better and nobler things. What in fact motivates the Soviet state is self-interest, coolly calculated and coolly carried through. It is too bad if an agreement on non-aggression is not in its interest; such a treaty would be somewhat shortlived. It would remain valid if, and only if, it falls in with the long-term objectives of the Soviet Union. A treaty would also be shortlived if the Soviet union within its own empire takes the law into its own hands and sets its armies on the march. In the end the *status quo* will be seen to be the predominant factor.

In those turbulent days none of the powers declared that an attack on the *status quo* represented a war situation. President Johnson renewed the Berlin guarantee. He declared that the Americans had made it unambiguously clear that the use of force or the threat of force in territories for which it held a measure of responsibility, such as Berlin, would not be tolerated.

That gave Foreign Minister Brandt an opportunity to declare how dangerous the Soviet claim was that it was in a position, on the basis of the Potsdam agreement or the UN Charter, to intervene unilaterally against a "threat of war" from the Federal Republic.

"Any attack against us," said Foreign Minister Brandt, "any military intervention in the Federal Republic would be an act of war. There is not the slightest doubt about this, not even for the Soviet Union. The governments of the three western powers have made this perfectly plain. For this reason I can say that we can feel as secure today under the protection of a treaty as we could a month ago or a year ago, and by 'we' I mean all members of the alliance and Berlin, and no one need have any fear on this score. . . ."

The drama of the Czech struggle for freedom was also translated by the Federal Republic into a myth of great national resistance, of holding out against impossible odds against brute force. A virtually unanimous resolution of the Federal parliament on 26 September 1968 was passed in respect of this national struggle for freedom.

Such were the principles upon which the policies of the Federal Republic had been based until then, but in Europe they were no longer viable. There was no power on earth prepared to chance its arm and practise brinkmanship in order to realise its objectives.

The Federal Minister for All-German Affairs expounded in the debate of 18 October 1968 the implications for Germany of the events in Czechoslovakia. It was evident, in his opinion, that the countries under Communist rule within the direct sphere of influence of Moscow were in a somewhat special position. For the Germans this was no mere academic question because this special position under the law also obtained for the other part of Germany. The leader of the FDP defied the flood of opinions and discord which dominated Germany after the occupation of Czechoslovakia, and on 14 December they demanded a realistic Ostpolitik, thereby paving the way towards the initiative which was taken up by Brandt's government. The spokesman said that the Federal Republic had to get used to the idea that the Soviet Union was also a partner in European politics, and very little could be achieved by opposing it. It would be as good as impossible to conduct an Ostpolitik which bypassed the GDR. The great adventure of a new initiative in German policies which the Federal Republic was to undertake in 1970 could already be detected in the guidelines laid down by an extraordinary meeting of the SPD. So one of the coalition parties in Kiesinger's government was putting forward a policy which contrasted sharply with that of the cabinet and took the following form: the Federal Republic needed a consistent policy to effect a balancing out of interests between the western and eastern alliances. The SPD intended to achieve this objective by means of co-operation between the Federal Republic and the GDR, and a non-aggression pact which might serve as a basis for mutual respect of frontiers until a peace treaty can be formulated. The SPD declared that the Munich agreement was invalid from the outset; but that care must be exercised to ensure that expellees suffer no harm because of this declaration of invalidity.

The following statement was made in the context of the reassessment of relations with the GDR:

> For us the GDR is not a foreign country. The Germans in the other part of our land are for us not a different nation. But it would be unreal to deny or to refuse to accept the existence of the other part of Germany as a state. On the other hand, in view of the fact that the leaders of the SED and GDR are not even prepared to consider entering into concrete negotiations on normalising conditions in Germany, the demands for recognition from the government of the GDR should not be taken as a constructive contribution to the regularisation of relations between the German states.

This resolution contains recognition of the existing boundaries "until such time as a peace treaty can be formulated," recognition of the Czech position with respect to the Munich agreement (that it was invalid from the outset), and provides for the institution of negotiations with the GDR at government level, working out a modus vivendi between the two German states, and normalisation of relations without recognition under international law.

"Respecting" of the frontier is the new formula established by Foreign Minister Brandt; it is not specific and could be interpreted in any number of ways. This is both an advantage and a disadvantage, because it binds one side too much and the other too little. "Respecting" could mean little more than the position which virtually all Germans associated themselves with, namely, not seeking to alter the frontier by force. Since force has been just about the only way frontiers have been altered throughout history renunciation of force implies respect of the frontier.

The associations of expellees, which were also committed to not changing the frontiers by force, also therefore "respected" them.

The First Secretary of the Polish Communist Party, Gomulka, took the view that Brandt's formula did not contain much that was positive. It was not enough for the Poles that the Germans could not take over the territories to the east of the Oder-Neisse line. If it had already gone beyond the point of a formal assertion, then only full recognition under the law would be of any value. Gomulka pointed out that the Federal Chancellor had not taken up his Foreign Minister's formulation. It was a step in the right direction, but fell far short of what was necessary. None the less the formula was potentially revisionist, because a definitive recognition of the German-Polish frontier would still remain an unresolved issue until such time as a peace conference settled it.

But Gomulka had at least expressed Poland's willingness to enter into a dialogue with the Federal Republic. And Foreign Minister Brandt took up the opportunity which was here being offered him. He took the view that reconciliation with Poland would be on a similar historical plane to reconciliation with France. He considered it possible that a solution of the frontier problem acceptable to both sides could be found even before the signing of a peace treaty.

Even at that time Brandt was putting the case for burying the old concept of unification. In the foreseeable future it was not possible to expect Germany to be united in a single state.

But the spirit of the so-called Hallstein doctrine was still to be felt in German politics. It came into effect at a time when the economic vitality of the Federal Republic was so evidently superior that it could claim to take the lead in German affairs, for the future of the GDR was still very much a question mark. At that time the notion that Germany would be permanently divided into two states was not far short of blasphemous.

On 30 May 1969 the Federal government resolved on a declaration of principle in the event of recognition of the GDR by other states. This declaration allowed it the possibility of a more flexible application of the Hallstein doctrine. But in essence the claim to sole representation remained unaltered.

The declaration draws attention to the fact that the right of the Federal government to act as representative for the entire German nation is already laid down in the constitution, whose preamble states that the Federal constitution also operates on behalf of those Germans who have been denied the possibility of co-operating in its creation. The final statement of the London nine-power conference which was held between 28 September and 3 October 1954 contains in its fifth section a common declaration from the governments of the three western powers which states that they—the USA, France and Great Britain—recognise the government of the Federal Republic as the sole German government, established freely and in accordance with legal principles, and which is therefore competent to speak for Germany as a whole in international dealings.

What was new now was that the Federal Republic no longer applied the Hallstein doctrine unthinkingly and automatically. Foreign Minister Brandt went as far as to say on 19 May 1969 that the Federal Government would regard it as "against the German interest" if two separate German ambassadors were to present themselves in certain world capitals.

But on the other hand the GDR should not be allowed a kind of sole representation in some capital cities if, as a result of recognition of the GDR the Federal Republic were to withdraw its own ambassador. Now and for the future the Federal Republic would no longer have to operate within a straitjacket. Federal Chancellor Kiesinger said in this context that establishment of diplomatic relations with the GDR must be regarded as an unfriendly act, because it was divisive and therefore operated counter to the stipulations of the constitution.

> If any country in the world recognises the régime over the border under international law this amounts to prejudgement, and prejudgement in a negative sense; it means taking a decision which it is up to the German people alone to make.
>
> Friendship and co-operation on a basis of mutual confidence is therefore only possible with those countries which on the fundamental issue of national unity stand on the side of the German people.

In the "Report on the state of the nation in a divided Germany," dated 17 June 1969 the Federal Chancellor repeated that "any kind of recognition of the GDR is impossible;" whereas the government which succeeded him, whilst stating that "real" recognition was impossible, was seeking for ways and means of finding "some kind of" recognition. Kiesinger was fundamentally opposed to the notion that the GDR was a state.

> The 17 millions living in the GDR do not regard themselves as citizens belonging to a state in the same way that the national populations of western Europe certainly do.... This is the fundamental difference between them and the peoples in the "Soviet camp." For they have not given their approval not only to the régime and the "constitution" which has been forced upon them but also to the very existence of a so-called second German state.... Recognition would be trying to make a right out of a wrong and would infringe against the universally recognised principle of self-determination. The Federal Republic has no right to take any such steps.

Klaus Schütz, the ruling mayor of Berlin, demanded on the other hand that the phantom of the "peace treaty" should be forgotten. The Germans must come to terms with the Poles on the basis of the *status quo* and not with regard to any possible future agreements which would only be temporarily valid until "the conclusion of peace." The character of the frontiers must be changed and transformed. This would represent a European solution of the frontier question.

> It does not postpone these problems to some indefinite time in the future, but states here and now: We want to proceed on the basis of the *status quo*, cause no harm to the integrity of any country, alter no frontiers, but we do seek to change the character of all the frontiers in Europe by means of a security system which brings peace to all and guarantees peace to all in Europe.

# BRANDT'S GOVERNMENT AND THE GDR: RECOGNITION BEFORE NEGOTIATION?

The Federal government, like its predecessor before it, declared its readiness to enter into binding agreements on mutual renunciation of the use or threat of force even with the GDR. The statement does not actually say that this agreement would be regarded as marking the end of negotiations and the coming of a modus vivendi with the GDR, but this can be adduced from the offer to negotiate sent to the GDR.

As former ruling mayor, Brandt knows better than anyone else that Berlin is the real test of the new Ostpolitik, and this is why he says a lot less about it than the others. If the Ostpolitik of the Federal government succeeds, then in the future the Federal Republic on the one hand and the states of eastern Europe on the other will be able to coexist within the framework of normal relations backed by treaty.

The only exception to this legally based and treaty-backed European system of states is Berlin, which will remain an outsider; there is no promise that efforts to bring an end to the "irregular and disorderly existence" of Berlin will meet with any success. The Russians must be sorely tempted to seek a comprehensive solution for Berlin as part of the "clean-up" campaign taking place under the cover of the non-aggression negotiations. For the city of West Berlin is an inescapable fact of life; and the new Ostpolitik of the Federal Republic gives the Soviet Union a chance to "make a fresh start" and "begin again from scratch." In the eyes of the Russians, West Berlin is a left-over from the Germany that collapsed once and for all in 1945 which will inevitably follow all the rest of the Reich into the abyss.

The declaration on Berlin in the government programme is therefore couched in the most undramatic of terms. It runs as follows:

> The Federal government will advise the USA, Great Britain and France to pursue with determination the discussions with the Soviet Union which have been instituted on the alleviation and improvement of the situation of Berlin. The status of the city of Berlin as a special responsibility of the four powers must remain unaltered. This should not prevent efforts being directed towards the improvement of communication links to Berlin. We shall continue to guarantee the viability of the city for the future. West Berlin must be given the opportunity of

> contributing to the improvement of political, economic and cultural relations in both parts of Germany.

All that is needed now is a link of some kind between the new arrangements with eastern Europe and the "securing of Berlin"; a commitment to the fact that the planned non-aggression treaties can only become a reality in conjunction with a definitive clarification of the position of Berlin.

The government has set about its task without any illusions, the declaration ends, thereby anticipating the difficulties, set-backs and disappointments of the coming year:

> Interests, power relationships and social differences can neither be solved dogmatically, nor should they be smoothed over. But those in dialogue with us must also recognise that the right of self-determination, as laid down in the Charter of the United Nations, also holds good for the German people. This right and our determination to maintain it can never be a subject of negotiation. We do not cherish the illusion that the work of reconciliation will be easily or rapidly concluded. It will take time, but the moment has now arrived to make a start.

For the CDU/CSU the possibilities Brandt is discussing are out of the question. In their view the GDR cannot be a party to negotiations about Germany. The opposition wants to appeal to the German people alone, and for them that means the population of the Federal Republic.

Former Federal Chancellor Kiesinger claims that the crucial sentence is missing from the government's declaration:

> This Federal government too regards itself as the sole German government which has been freely, legally and democratically elected and which is therefore mandated to speak for the whole German nation.

Kiesinger's statement takes the line that a dialogue between the two German states will not yield any results, "neither in recognising the realities nor in improvement of relationships with either the western or eastern world, nor indeed in improving our relations with the other part of Germany." He continues:

> Consider that what we label the second German state is a reference to a situation such as exists nowhere else in the world. Opinions may differ as to whether you can really give the name of state to a situation, a phenomenon, a system . . . where people rule without legality, without a mandate. I am aware that opinions differ widely on this score. Over there—in that other part of Germany—there is really no such thing as a day-by-day expression of grass roots opinion. The people over there are forced to act as they do by masters to whose position of authority they have not given their approval. . . . Over there the people do not regard themselves as the citizens of a particular state but as a part of

the German nation as a whole which aspires to live together with us in a single German state.

In addition the masters in the other part of Germany do not even exercise power on their own authority nor can they carry out their policies in the way they think fit, but they live and rule by courtesy of the Communist superpower in Europe.

There may well be a lot of truth in this, but it completely excludes any possibility of negotiation and agreement with the GDR. No government, unless acting under the severest pressure, will negotiate if it is not recognised as a government representative of its people but regarded as having usurped power. It is not possible to maintain any kind of relations with anyone whose right to exist and to be respected is disputed. If the régime in the other part of Germany cannot really be regarded as a government in a position to negotiate, if one follows the strong inclinations of every freedom-loving individual to regard the GDR in the same terms as Kurt Georg Kiesinger does, then all that one can do is to wait for the day on which justice and freedom emerge victorious against injustice, enslavement and unnatural partition through forces from within.

But German history since 1945 has not worked like that. National consciousness has grown up like a natural force to counter partition. The unity of the German nation has become weaker, and the two German states have become stronger and more confident. The population of the Federal Republic hardly think of their state as a temporary institution; it has become for them—as the GDR has become for its population—the basis and physical context of their lives.

It demands an excess of confidence to exclaim, as does Kiesinger, that the Federal government is not in a position to enter into any agreements on the German-Polish frontier. "That is a matter for the German people as a whole."

But the continued existence of the Federal Republic is itself evidence enough against "waiting for the great day," against an attitude which would reserve the important decisions until the restoration of a unified Germany which alone would be competent to resolve them. The Federal Republic came into being because decisions on the economic form and social pattern of the German people could no longer be held in abeyance until victor and vanquished agreed on the structure of Germany. The Federal Republic was founded upon the courage to build for the future without guarantees of permanence, without waiting until Germany rose up again and an all-German state could make its peace. The great treaties of the Federal Republic with the western powers have "anticipated" that peace on many crucial issues. The whole of

German existence, whether in the Federal Republic or the GDR, was a "peace in anticipation of the armistice."

The foreign policy of Brandt's government is reasserted, explained and justified in the "Report on the state of the nation" which the Chancellor delivered on 14 January 1970. This report reveals the pattern of Brandt's policy in relation to Germany; it is an outline of the development of the German question in 1970, a strategy for the game of Germany which the Federal government was to conduct in 1970.

Once more Brandt puts his finger on the two basic facts of the German situation: the German nation, which has remained unbroken, and the two states, which have appeared to replace the Reich and which after twenty-five years remain the sole political realities on German soil.

> Twenty-five years after the unconditional surrender of the Hitler Reich the concept of the German nation is the bond which holds a divided Germany together. The concept of nationhood unites historical reality and political will. "Nation" means more than a common language and culture, more than a state and a social order. The nation is founded upon an enduring sense of community among the individuals that make it up. No one can deny that a German nation in this sense of the term exists and will continue to exist for the foreseeable future.
>
> Of course, in the two social and political structures which have now been in existence on German territory for more than two decades, utterly opposed and irreconcilable views have been expressd as to what form the unification of Germany and a common future should take and how this objective is to be attained. Let no one cherish the vain hope of being able to avoid the disputes which are inevitable because two totally different kinds of society coexist on German territory. On this issue we are agreed with Ulbricht: between our system and the one which has grown up to the east there can be no hybrid, no simple compromise.

The two systems are irreconcilable and incompatible—such is the basic premise that underpins the government's policy on Germany as a whole; it is possible neither to unite nor merge the two; therefore there will in the foreseeable future be no one single state for Germany, no reunification.

Nor can this objective be hoped for through some kind of decline on the part of the GDR. The permanence of the GDR as a state in the other part of Germany is a reality that must be accepted. Acceptance is not recognition; to take cognisance of something is not the same thing as agreeing with it and awarding it a "seal of approval." Reality is the here and now, and our projection of the future, so far as this is possible. To accept something as a reality does not mean giving up the hope of being able to change it in the course of time.

Brandt develops his train of thought by stating that new avenues must be explored; the obvious, dramatic solutions to the German question no longer held good, not even within the context of the nation itself. Now only one kind of solution remained: the gradual construction of an international system.

> It is my conviction that there will in the future be no more political solutions of any substance which will not take the form of alliances, security systems or communities. The important German questions will in the future not be settled on the basis of the nation state in the traditional sense, but only in step-by-step movement towards a European peace system. Therefore it is necessary for us to recognise the realities of the situation and to respect them—this does not mean enduring existing injustices passively, but making a positive and practical contribution over the years towards removing from international frontiers the notion that they merely divide states.

The Federal Chancellor urged parliament and the German people not to forget one fact, despite all the difficulties and unpleasant realities of the situation, namely, that the world at large does not regard the re-emergence of a German state of 77 million people as in its best interest. There should be no doubt about the fact that outside Germany there were not all that many people who were enthusiastic at the prospect that the two German states, which were 60 million and 17 million strong respectively, let alone their combined industrial and military potential, might join forces. But nowadays it was a prospect hardly worth fighting over. "Still I want to make clear what I believe to be the truth in this regard, that despite everything the unity of the nation still exists."

The nation is however not something to be taken for granted, as something that appears by spontaneous generation and is handed to the Germans on a plate as a kind of divine right. This unity of the German people should rather be regarded as a process, Brandt continued, "whose opportunities can also be thrown away—for they are opportunities, nothing more."

Brandt has convincingly demonstrated his resolve to maintain the ties between the Federal Republic and the western world. The free part of Germany must remain free; that is one of the fundamental principles which Brandt laid down as part of the German policy of his government. He expresses it tellingly in terms of the Germans' need to "recognise themselves." It is one of Brandt's basic tenets that the military ties between the Federal Republic and the western world are an absolute necessity. Thus he is scotching the old fiction that the rearmament of the two Germanies would once more give the Germans the chance to unleash the hounds of war. "The Federal army is not capable of undertaking military initiatives on its own account. . . . The strike forces of the

GDR are not in a position to undertake military action on their own authority outside the framework of the eastern pact system."

He had not the least intention "to flit from one side to the other." Even former Federal Chancellor Kiesinger vouches for the fact that Brandt has no intention of conducting a conspiratorial Ostpolitik like many people in the Weimar Republic who tried to make Germany the pointer on the scales between east and west in the sense that, swinging to and fro unfettered by any alliance obligations, the country could one day opt for the west and the next for the east. In its tussle with the Chancellor, the opposition rooted out a statement by Schumacher on the illusory nature of the idea that Germany was a halfway post between east and west.

> In our policies we must also beware of slipping back into the evangelical delusion of the bridge theory. Those were illusions which in 1933 were born of the hope of arriving at a compromise with a totalitarian opponent who coveted everything which would allow the retention of political existence and independence.

In the debate the word "Rapallo" keeps recurring. The Federal Chancellor does not think it worth the effort to spell out the fact that his policies resemble the Rapallo Treaty about as much as the Treaty of Germany resembles the Versailles Treaty, about as much as the Marshall Plan, whose aim was to reconstruct German industry, does the "reparations," which sought to destroy it; as much as the Federal army, created to meet the Soviet threat, resembles the Reich army, which concluded a secret pact with the Red Army, in order to circumvent the Versailles Treaty by means of poison gas and munitions factories, airfields and machines of war on Soviet territory.

Rapallo was an accommodation between two defeated parties and was a result of the anxiety of the Reich government at the prospect of becoming involved in a war of sanctions against the Soviet Union and thereby becoming the most advanced and thus the most threatened outpost on the sanctions front line. The Reich did not want to become the mustering point of the west against the Soviet Union. Thanks to Hitler's crazy war on two fronts it has become the mustering point for both the western and Russian armies. On the other side of the coin, a war of sanctions against the Soviet Union is no longer on the cards, because in the United Nations every big power can prevent sanction measures against itself by using its veto. Roosevelt deliberately introduced the veto, giving as his reason the fact that the UN would only be able to force a nation to its knees by means of economic sanctions if it were unable to defend itself militarily, for such measures taken against countries which were capable of defending themselves would mean war. Any comparison with Rapallo is the most twisted kind of anachronism possible. The Ostpolitik of Brandt resembles Rapallo as much as the occupied, divided Germany of 1970 resembles the free Weimar Republic with its all-German government and all-German army.

In the year 1921, the year of the Rapallo Treaty, it would have been regarded as a lunatic delusion to imagine that one day two German states would negotiate with each other, that there would be two German capitals, one in Brandenburg and one in the Rhineland. Even more fantastic would have been the notion that these two Germanies would confront one another for twenty years and communicate only through slanging matches, and that, separated one from the other by barbed wire emplacements like a no man's land in trench warfare, they would stand opposed to each other like hostile armies during a truce. The Federal Chancellor now refers to this background when he says: "Negotiations must, can and will finally take place between Bonn and East Berlin." Anyone who brings to mind this background will inevitably be both moved and excited by these words. They sound like the signal proclaiming the armistice after a twenty-year long war, although some will regard the fanfare as heralding victory, others as bringing defeat. The Federal Chancellor was thinking neither of the one nor of the other. In the battle between freedom and enslavement there would, he knew, never be an armistice.

In negotiations with East Berlin there would be certain "fixed points of reference:" the right to self-determination, the struggle towards national unity and freedom within the context of a European peace system, continued links with West Berlin, without prejudice to the responsibility of the four powers for Berlin as a whole.

> The Federal government respects—and will continue to respect—the rights and responsibilities which the three powers have with regard to Germany as a whole and Berlin in particular. It is not in our minds to undermine this situation, nor to let others undermine it. I have worked long enough in Berlin to know that there are burdens which our shoulders are not broad enough to carry alone and which it is not in the interest of the Federal Republic to seek unrestricted sovereignty.

For the negotiations with East Berlin Brandt established six basic principles:

> 1. Both states have their obligations to preserve the unity of the German nation. Neither should regard the other as a foreign country.
> 2. For the rest, the generally recognised principles of international law hold good, especially the exclusion of any kind of discrimination, respect of territorial integrity, the obligation to resolve all matters of

dispute in a peaceful manner and mutual respect of common frontiers.
3. This also implies an obligation not to seek to change the social structure in the territory of the other partner to the treaty by force.
4. The two governments and those acting in their name should work towards neighbourly collaboration, especially in establishing scientific and technical co-operation.
5. The existing rights and responsibilities of the four powers in relation to Germany as a whole and Berlin must be respected.
6. The efforts of the four powers to arrive at an improvement in the position in and around Berlin must be supported.

The Federal Chancellor is aware that the GDR is resolved not to offer anything in return for Federal recognition of a fact of life and of an indisputable claim to independence under international law.

The Chancellor conceded that the Federal Republic would probably have to make concessions in advance. But the concessions which had once been made to the west had, in Brandt's generous words, repaid themselves in full.

> There was a time in the Federal Republic when substantial German concessions to the west were considered to be proof positive of especial political acumen and farsightedness. And in fact it can now readily be seen that this has largely paid off for the Federal Republic in terms of the trust, equality of rights and non-discrimination we have gained for ourselves.

It would therefore be both petty and unpatriotic to ask, he continued, if the same approach is tried in the east, "What do we get in return?"

> To make a securer peace for our people as a whole—is that nothing? To set alongside friendship with the peoples of the west, north, and south, confidence, agreement and perhaps one day friendship as well with the peoples in the east—is that nothing? And will Germany not be more secure and have a more lasting peace? Will its people not profit by this, every single one of them? Let me put it this way: because there will be less fear, because the burdens will become lighter, because people who have not seen each other for years will be able to meet again, because it will perhaps be possible for two people from the two German states, which are now so inhumanely divided, to marry one another. Those are the objectives, both large and small, but always concerned with human beings, which this government sets itself in all earnestness with full awareness of the difficulties, the length of the way ahead, and the risks which have been properly calculated. This is the task we are able to set ourselves, because we are confident and have good friends.

It is a great undertaking for men to reach out to one another despite the conflict between the state systems which, in Brandt's words, will never come to an end.

In the speech which Kiesinger delivered in answer to Brandt's report on the state of the nation, there can be detected a certain measure of consensus.

Kiesinger now regarded an understanding between the Poles and the Germans on the Oder-Neisse line as on the cards even before the coming of a peace treaty.

> The question of the Oder-Neisse line will only really be able to be resolved in a peace treaty; but this does not present us from sitting round the table and trying to find a solution acceptable to both peoples and also acceptable to later generations—for our country is also our children's country.

Kiesinger stated that for him too the fate of the people in the GDR was of greater concern to him than reunification.

> We have urged you to approach Herr Ulbricht with specific proposals. We are prepared to give you our support in this. What form might the proposals take? They should be similar to Konrad Adenauer's formula that we have a great deal we could talk about if conditions in the zone became more humane. We associate ourselves with this view; for we too recognise that the freedom of our fellow countrymen in the zone and a dignified life for them means more than a mere mechanical joining together of the divided parts of Germany.

However, Kiesinger added, the "alternative" between freedom for the population of the GDR and reunification is not a real one. "Give the people over there freedom and the result will be reunification," he declared.

Students of the GDR doubt that. This is what Richert writes in his book *Das andere Deutschland* (The other Germany):

> A measure of fairness in conditions at work and in life generally, a realistic system of incentives and opportunities, positive recognition of specialist achievement, preferably in the form of enhanced social prestige, can all serve to prepare the common ground on which the interests of the leadership and the population can meet.

In this way "there can be established a meeting between rulers and ruled on a practical level."

The west triumphs if the SED complains that its young people, totally opposed to ideologies, lack the social consciousness which the administration and welfare function of the state took for granted. The conclusion of the west would be: "They belong to us. That is why they are not doing it."

> If things are allowed to continue in that way there will in all probability be little more to do in the way of unification in forty years' time,

> when the present younger generation has become the generation of the old.

There was quite a battle over what the GDR, the more mysterious half of a mystifying Germany, would then become.

In the Federal parliament and in the nation at large the point at issue was whether the GDR was a state and whether the Federal Republic and the GDR were, by origin and nature, fundamentally opposed structures—and therefore worlds apart. What Professor Carlo Schmid had to say on this score in the Federal parliament was illuminated by the great debate which flared up again in 1970 concerning the nature of Germany and the historical appearance of the two German states. Professor Schmid, one of the creators of the Federal constitution, demonstrated how much his own views had shifted.

> In the creation of the constitution, the Federal Republic was regarded in the first instance as no more than a temporary institution, as a mere transitional state. In the intervening period between then and now, things have taken place which have caused this temporary institution to take on permanent statehood—that is, from the point of view of the material attributes of a state, and if one does not ask too penetrating questions about sovereignty in the fullest meaning of the word.

In those early days, Schmid continued, it would have been as inappropriate to call the Federal Republic a state as it would the GDR, but now things have changed beyond recognition. Carlo Schmid asked:

> Is the GDR today still only a "shell," a passing phenomenon? Is it not something which can lay claim to the title of "state"? In all concepts of the state, the state is defined as follows: a state can be said to exist where there is a population, a territory and a central authority. The moral and democratic quality of this state is irrelevant. Under "population" we do not mean the free population in the sense of Rousseau which determines the form of its own state, but simply the people who live within its territorial authority and, freely or involuntarily, are prepared to obey this authority. The definition is as crude as that. If it is only possible for a state to be a state if it is conducted on democratic lines and where human rights operate, then the Soviet Union is not a state.

Both German states came into being in the same way. Neither is an expression of the German people's right to self-determination. "Our origins, like those of the GDR, are the product of one phase in Allied military occupation policy. But in contrast to the GDR we acquired the opportunity of becoming democratic Germans in our part of Germany." He continues:

> But that does not alter the fact that across the frontier another state actually exists. These two states form the parts of the German nation; for the population of these two states—taken both as individuals and as a whole—wish it to be so. . . . But neither of the two states is the same as the Reich was; they are both new systems that have grown up on their own base, systems formulated in a period of transition, systems which have their present form because other powers who ruled over us wished it to be so.

The Federal Chancellor repeated what he had intimated in the parliamentary debate in an interview on American television on 16 January; namely, that reunification in the established sense had become an impossibility.

> I falter when I hear this word, especially the first syllable "re-". It gives the impression that things have to return to some previous stage. That will not happen. In no circumstances could it happen. I believe in the unity of our people, but it does not have to be realised in the context of a national state.

The Federal government's declaration that recognition of the GDR under international law was out of the question was somewhat diluted by the chairman of the SPD parliamentary party, Herbert Wehner, in an interview with the weekly *Der Spiegel*. This also forms part of the picture of the debate over Germany. Apparently fixed notions are subject to constant change and keep reappearing under ever-shifting guises.

The *Spiegel* interviewer had suggested that the policies of the Federal government, whether they wanted to or no, were moving in the direction of ultimate recognition of the GDR, and that the government would always have to be facing this reproach. To this Wehner replied: "I have nothing against it. Recognition under international law is not an absolute act." Perhaps the Federal Republic would have to "help to bring a situation into being" in which the question of recognition took on a different aspect. The *Spiegel* interviewer then summarised Wehner's statements, and he accepted the summary:

> If certain changes were to manifest themselves in the eastern situation as a whole, changes whose possible appearance we cannot predict today but which would seem to us to be positive, then perhaps even the question of recognition under international law might emerge in a new light.

By the end of 1970 such changes had not begun to take place. So the Brandt government had not so far translated possible recognition of the GDR into one of their practical policies. It has refused this recognition for as long as this has meant giving up recognising the German nation.

For the present, the GDR has only wanted to speak about Germany in terms of announcing its death, and only offers to negotiate in order to tear the ground from under its feet, for in the eyes of the GDR the two German states had become independent under international law and had ceased to be "German" states whose actions and dealings had any relation to the nation as a whole.

On 20 January 1970 the chairman of the GDR council of state declared that his government was ready to negotiate, but that recognition of the GDR under international law was a necessary prior condition. The basis must be the conclusions of the Potsdam agreement, which should be regarded as definitive international law. The Federal government replied with this declaration:

> The Federal government operates on the assumption that the GDR will conduct itself in the same manner as the Soviet Union and Poland. It is customary for treaties to come only as a result of negotiations and not as a precondition of negotiations.

None the less, the Federal government proposed on 22 January 1970 that negotiations be initiated "on the exchange of declarations on non-aggression."

> Such negotiations, to be conducted on the basis of non-discrimination, should offer the opportunity for a broadly-based exchange of views on means for the solution of all the outstanding issues between our two states, among them relations on a basis of mutual equality.

The Federal Chancellor stated in the note to the chairman of the GDR council of ministers that he regarded as the objective of the negotiations "to arrive at solutions to practical questions which would result in improving the quality of life for the populations of a divided Germany."

The reply of the GDR Prime Minister—Stoph proposed discussions with the Federal Chancellor in the GDR seat of government in Berlin—sounded more like an order. It virtually amounted to a request to Chancellor Brandt to appear in the office of the Prime Minister of the GDR on 16 or 27 September at 11 o'clock.

Detailed preparations for the talks threatened to come adrift because of a fundamental difference of opinion on a factual issue. The eastern side raised the strongest possible protest against Brandt's proposed route via West Berlin. A declaration of the ministerial council of the GDR dated 10 March based its objections on the need for the Federal Chancellor to avoid any political demonstration against the GDR if he wished to enter into equal negotiations with that country. West Berlin is not part of the Federal Republic of Germany but is a separate political entity. It lies on the territory of the GDR and it owes its existence only to the acquiescence of the GDR which tolerates foreign occupation there and has accepted the many incursions of the Federal Republic into West Berlin. The principle of equality of rights demands that "Herr Brandt as leader of his government should on the occasion of his meeting with the other party to the negotiations respect the sovereignty of the GDR and on his journey there respect the sovereign rights of the GDR in regard to the principles of international law."

The Federal government considered it unwise to engage in a trial of strength and suggested another location for negotiations. The incident was not a good omen: the Federal government had stumbled across an almost fanatical unwillingness to move on the question of Berlin; there seemed little prospect of loosening the stranglehold on Berlin.

On 17 March 1970 the heads of government of the GDR and the Federal Republic met in Erfurt. It was no small occurrence that their leaders were meeting for the first time since the foundation of the two states. But it was only a meeting on the surface; they came together like two heralds delivering proclamations drawn up in advance. Both sides read out prepared statements. As the host, the Prime Minister of the GDR had the first word. Proposal by proposal, sentence by sentence, word by word, he turned down everything the Federal government had proposed.

> Our two states bear the joint responsibility for ensuring that war will never again break out on German territory. In a few weeks will come the twenty-fifth anniversary of the day on which the German Reich—which was fashioned out of blood and iron—suffered defeat through blood and iron. The highest and most humane obligation of our two states is the prevention of a recurrence of that horror.

In the form of words "the most humane obligation" the GDR had found a counter-slogan to "improving the quality of life." The humanity of a secure peace was far more important than lightening the individual lot, and recognition of the GDR under international law was the best means of achieving this objective. But the Federal government would link "counter-revolutionary" intentions with such a fundamental and historical act; that is what Stoph called what in the proposals of the Federal government was described as "improving the quality of life" which, at least in the early stages, would inevitably throw a spanner in the works of the GDR.

The relations between the Federal Republic and the GDR would have to repose on the basis of the full sovereignty of the two German states. "Inter-German relations," in the way the Federal Republic was talking of them, amounts to giving the GDR stewardship and is no more than a disguised form of the claim to sole representation. The GDR has already suffered enough, the statement continues, in "inter-German relations," namely by an economic war against the GDR which derived from the Federal Republic's claims of domination and denial of the GDR. Stoph hoped that the Federal Republic would make compensation for the loss caused (totalling 1,000 million marks).

The GDR was not after inter-German relations, because the interests of the workers and of socialism far outweighed any supposed common national concerns.

> You yourself, Federal Chancellor, have stated that there can be "no half measures, no empty compromise" between the two diametrically opposed social systems in the GDR and the Federal Republic. And indeed this is true, the two sovereign German states cannot be united, because diametrically opposed social orders cannot be brought together.

This line of thought was logical and could not be faulted; Stoph stated that nothing need be paid for the recognition of an indisputable claim under international law and a state to which the future of Germany belonged.

Stoph then presented the treaty draft which Ulbricht, the Chairman of the council of state had sent to the Federal Chancellor and proposed that immediate discussions take place upon it. Recognition under international law could very swiftly be completed; it would all be over in a flash.

What the Federal Chancellor had in mind could not be dealt with in a few moments. He was contemplating a whole range of measures which could serve to improve the lot of the population and establish a network of contacts and scientific and technical collaboration. This would require much administrative work and detailed planning. The treaty Stoph was thinking of could be written on a single sheet; the agreements that could result from the Chancellor's ideas would have filled a large volume.

Brandt was concerned with the inner unity of the nation. When the nation had apparently fallen into decay after total defeat in war there had been, so the Chancellor argued in his presentation of the historical situation, an opportunity for a new beginning. But the rise of Germany did not take place through a single German state, but within and through two separate states. These were realities that had to be respected and taken into consideration. But they were not the only realities on German territory; the German nation was still a reality; and no policies could survive which did not take account of this reality.

> We cannot simply undo the division of Germany. But we can do our utmost to mitigate its consequences and take positive steps in the direction of bridging the gulf which separates us within Europe and

> that means within Germany too. And my basis for advance is the continuing and living reality of a German nation. I am free of any nationalist illusions that belong to a past age. But I am more than confident that national elements will themselves not lose their validity in the path twoards European and world-wide federation. The strong ties of a past which we have experienced together and for which we are jointly responsible, ties which no one can ignore, the ties of the family, of language, of culture and all those imponderable qualities which make us feel part of the same community—these too are a reality. A policy which would seek to deny or ignore this cornerstone of our national existence would in my estimation be doomed to failure.

Brandt continued by stating that the citizens of the two Germanies were realistic enough to know that even when the same spirit moved both sides, the two leaders would not be in a position to achieve a unified state. The world situation would not permit this. But the relations between the two states constituted a special relationship; and indeed in a negative sense, because they "have been suppressed in both parts of Germany to a level beneath that at which foreign states and their citizens deal with one another."

It is, Brandt maintained, the duty of the statesman to take the realities into consideration; but he should not select only that aspect of reality that suited him. The existence of West Berlin and its links with the west are just as much realities as the two Germanies. In any event, the Federal government regarded "efforts towards normalisation and reduction of tension to the east as indissolubly bound up with similar efforts in and around Berlin."

The Federal Chancellor repeated the basic principles which had already been presented in the Federal parliament with regard to the negotiations between the GDR and the Federal Republic which had now been instituted.

The Federal government, he stated, did not have a counter-draft to set against the treaty document which had been put before it. The objective of the exchange of views in Erfurt should not be the immediate conclusion of a treaty, but rather the purpose should be to establish

> whether it is possible for us to enter into negotiations which might conclude with a settlement by treaty of the relations between the Federal Republic and the GDR. For my government it is a matter of course that a treaty or agreement between us would have to have the same binding force as any agreement which we conclude with other states.

Again and again the contrast becomes evident between the GDR which is mainly after a document giving the GDR recognition under international law, and the objectives of the Federal Republic, whose aim it is to improve the conditions of the German people.

Formal documents alone are not enough to normalise relationships; ordinary people must have a taste of "normalisation" and see it at work in their everyday lives.

The signing of the legal document is just the first step; treaties must not be allowed "to remain an empty shell."

Moreover, Brandt states in all honesty that "in my opinion a genuine normalisation must be a contributory factor towards doing away with inter-German frontier fortifications and the wall."

Both German states would have to work towards the goal of a special mutual relationship; their mutual dealings could only exist within a special framework; the general formula of "recognition under international law" did not hold good for the special case of the relationship between the GDR and the Federal Republic. Up until now the relationship had been "special" in a negative sense; and agreement over the establishment of relations on the basis of equality must also be "special" in nature. Brandt brushed the claim to sole representation emphatically to one side: "Neither side can act as the other's keeper. I have not come to Erfurt to demand that certain social structures be done away with."

Brandt parried Stoph's question as to whether he was ready to negotiate with the words: "We are ready to find out if the time is ripe."

Brandt does not conceal the fact that the GDR and the Federal Republic are divided by substantial differences of opinion on the meaning and objective of an understanding between the two states. Brandt pointed out that the constitutions of the two states and their treaties of alliance retain the possibility of Germany as a united state. Nothing is likely to alter this attitude, and therefore the notions of recognition under international law and non-intervention in internal affairs were not relevant to the establishment of relations between the two states on a basis of equality. For the principles on which a treaty between the two states might rest should not exclude the prospect that the will of the German people might make itself heard.

Therefore the Chancellor was not ready to conclude right away general treaty documents containing fine-sounding declarations of principle but no real decisions. He repeatedly stressed the fact that they should lower their sights. For this reason he recommended the establishment of a commission to work out practical measures for the improvement of relations between the two states.

In conclusion the Federal Chancellor proposed to the Prime Minister of the GDR the continuation of discussions in the near future, this time on west German territory.

On 20 March the Federal Chancellor reported to the Federal parliament on the results of the Erfurt conversations; at the beginning of his speech, Brandt stated that "the journey to Erfurt was right and necessary," and continued:

> On the other hand, it was clear from the very outset that Erfurt could provide only the first steps in an exchange of views which would bring to light the profound differences between the two states. No one expected that apart from general statements on the securing of peace and on the discussion of a handful of practical measures, a meeting of minds would be possible, and no one did expect this. Erfurt could be no more than a beginning. And it was such a beginning.

He had, he said, set himself no higher objective than that this first meeting should be followed by a second. In any case, he could see no way in which a real meeting of minds on basic issues would be possible.

> The government of the GDR concentrates solely on recognition as it understands the term, without recognising the positive changes it proposes for German coexistence and for cooperation between the two states in Germany. The GDR government also presented a string of demands which cannot be met because they lack either a legal or moral basis.

The Federal Chancellor repeated to the Federal parliament his answer to the question posed by the GDR Prime Minister as to what the actual objectives of his policy towards the GDR were:

> I have sought to explain to him that we naturally had no aggressive intentions, but aspired towards neighbourly collaboration; that we sought peaceful coexistence between the two German states; but at the same time we must all avoid anything which would permanently inhibit the chance that one day, however remote that day may be, the German people would be able in free self-determination to decide upon the political framework of their mutual co-operation within the context of a European peace.

Federal President Heinemann's address to the diplomatic corps on the occasion of the twenty-fifth anniversary of the end of the war also marked a substantial contribution to the dialogue with the east. The President stated that the Federal Republic was making a solemn confession of faith and completing the process of self-recognition.

> In looking back over the past twenty-five years we should recognise the effort required to take a demoralised population in devastated cities and millions of homeless and penniless refugees and create on such a basis a peaceful and democratic society which, despite the great sacrifices it has had to make, despite the fact that the unity of our nation has ben torn apart, has none the less remained immune against sentiments of hatred or revenge.
>
> It should be recognised that the overwhelming majority of our

> citizens reacted differently from 1918 and did not yield to the temptations of a new shortsighted nationalism, but directed themselves towards the concept of European solidarity and collaboration among all nations. This is today the basis of the political philosophy of a people who have learned to contemplate their own destiny with sober dignity.

According to Heinemann, the Germans bore a special responsibility for the creation of peace in Europe. The present endeavours of the Federal Republic must be recognised as part of the efforts towards carrying out this German responsibility.

> The Erfurt meeting has shown that this responsibility, unlike our country, cannot be divided. One of the enduring points in common among all people in Germany is the conviction and firm resolve that war will never again originate on German soil. This is the only way we can continue to live on in the face of the senseless deaths of all those victims of the last war and the terror.

The second meeting between the two leaders, which took place in Kassel, showed more clearly even than the Erfurt meeting how far apart the two sides really were. More than in Erfurt the emotions of the cold war obtruded into the sessions. Many of the measures taken in this underhand war still persisted. At the beginning of the conference, Stoph made strong protests over the legal proceedings pending in the Federal Republic against politicians in the GDR. The GDR also objected because the Federal Republic did not support the GDR application for membership of the World Health Organisation.

In reply, the Federal Chancellor declared that a genuine rapprochement between the two states must occur before the Federal Republic could feel able to support the GDR in the world at large. A formal and legalistic document would not of itself bring about a closer relationship between the two German states, particularly if it just served to retain their separate identities. In the constitutions of the two states the unity of the nation was stated as a deeper level underlying the two states. The two constitutions were based on the intention that the division of Germany was to be purely temporary, and that any agreement between the GDR and the Federal Republic must lower barriers and not render them any more permanent. Treaty agreements must of course be concluded on the basis of equality of rights and non-discrimination, but they must also have a concrete purpose, "which would genuinely signify an advance in our relations and in the lives of Germans in all Germany." A treaty between the two German states should not seek to "skate round" the rights of the four victorious powers. Brandt confessed that he could not believe that the demand for formal recognition was all that the GDR government had to bring forward. In Erfurt there had been no time to introduce proper negotiations. This was why he was now putting forward principles and treaty clauses for the institution of relations between the two German states on a basis of equality.

> 1. The Federal Republic of Germany and the German Democratic Republic, whose constitutions are aimed at the unity of the nation, conclude in the interest of peace as well as of the future and coherence of the nation this treaty which shall serve as the basis for relations between the two states in Germany, for improving the links between the two states and which shall contribute to removing existing disadvantages.

The second Clause provides for the fact that the treaty would have to be approved by the legislative assemblies of the two states.

> 3. The two sides shall declare their intent to conduct their relations on the basis of human rights, equality, peaceful coexistence and non-discrimination which are the general principles governing international law.

Clause Four obligates both states to the peaceful resolution of disputes. Among these are included the settlement of frontier questions and territorial integrity.

In this way the Federal Republic was fulfilling its pledge to exchange non-aggression declarations with the GDR. But the non-aggression pact was contained within a treaty which was outside the framework of international law. And the Federal Republic insisted on concluding a treaty on inter-German relations on a basis of equality between the two German states, which alone would set the relations between them on a regular footing. This fourth clause did not impose any new obligations on the Federal Republic because it was already bound by the terms of the Treaty of Germany not to change the frontier with the GDR by force. Non-aggression, as incorporated into a treaty on inter-German relations, did not reach out into the chill air of relations under international law.

The GDR did not insist on non-aggression declarations before taking up diplomatic relations. It wanted to make a declaration of non-aggression from the heights of international sovereignty and turn it into a victory of the power which put an end to Germany.

> 5. Both sides respect the independence and sovereignty of each of the two German states in matters of internal sovereignty.

The notion of "internal sovereignty" was a reservation and a limitation. According to it there was another kind of sovereignty which did not lie exclusively with the two German states, but with the Allies and above all with the German people as a whole.

Clause Six lays down that neither state can act for the other as its representative. This is the clearest possible renunciation of the concept of sole representation.

Under Clause Seven the two states declare that war must never be permitted to begin again on German territory.

Under Clause Eight the two states undertake "to refrain from any actions which are aimed at interrupting peaceful coexistence between the peoples."

Under Clause Nine the two states affirm their intention to support all efforts towards disarmament control which are in the interests of increasing European security.

The tenth Cause is more a declaration of principle than part of a treaty agreement. It states that there are two states in existence on German territory, but that their citizens feel themselves to be members of one nation. The purpose of this clause is to affirm that one does not exclude the other. "The existence of two German states" does not mean at all that the German nation is no more, that it has ceased to exist because the Germans are no longer united under a single state; and the continued existence of the German nation does not mean that the reality and the claim to existence on the part of the two German states can be brushed aside.

The eleventh Clause lays down that the current obligations of the two Germanies towards the Allies should remain untouched, insofar as they relate to "the special rights and agreements of the powers on Berlin and Germany as a whole."

That is a reference back to the days when the control commission embodied "Germany as a whole." After it broke down and Germany was divided into zones of occupation, the Germans followed on and became divided into two German states. Since they themselves were not in a position to restore unity, only the continuing responsibility of the victorious powers towards Germany as a whole remained as a hope that the remnants of their national existence would be preserved.

> Clause 12. The four-power agreements on Berlin and Germany are to be respected. The same holds good for the links which have come into being between West Berlin and the Federal Republic of Germany. Both sides undertake to support the efforts of the four powers towards normalising the situation in and around Berlin.

Clause Thirteen seeks to prevent direct conflict between the legislation of the two states, whose right of sovereignty is none the less regarded as restricted to their respective territorial areas.

Clause Fourteen provides for measures for the increase of inter-state travel and freedom of movement.

Clause Fifteen deals with reuniting families.

Clause Sixteen seeks to allow parishes and local areas on the common frontier to resolve problems in a neighbourly manner.

Clause Seventeen proceeds from the willingness of the two states to step up co-operation in every possible area (travel, post, exchange of information, science, culture, environmental questions, sport, etc.).

Clause Eighteen deals with the building up of trade.

In Clause Nineteen provision is made for the nomination of delegates by both sides in order to form a kind of standing commission in both capitals.

In Clause Twenty the two states undertake to facilitate membership and collaboration in international organisations on the basis of the treaty which is to be agreed by them.

The discussion in Kassel was rendered more difficult because the Prime Minister of the GDR, Stoph, scarcely paid any attention to the declarations of the Federal Republic regarding recognition of the frontiers and territorial integrity of the GDR. Anything less than recognition of the GDR under international law, he maintained, produces the danger of international conflict at the most explosive spot on the European map.

> Anyone who leaves open the basic questions of war or peace between the great military groups is constantly inducing the danger of serious conflict situations which only increase tension rather than reducing it.

It was remarkable, he continued, that the Federal Republic should talk about improving the conditions of people and yet resist the highest command of humanity, recognition under international law. That could only mean that the Federal Republic wanted to keep the back door open for violence.

> Refusal to give the GDR and its frontiers recognition under international law compels us to draw the conclusion that the option is being left open of taking aggressive action against the frontiers of the GDR, its state system and social order, on the assumption that by so doing the aggressor will not be held responsible for his aggression.

The GDR sought a just solution. The basic and fundamental issues would have to be resolved.

> In the present situation, the establishment of any kind of commission or delegate body which would begin with the discussion of secondary or even less important issues before the achievement of an agreement in principle between the two heads of government on the institution of relations under international law on a basis of equality would serve little purpose and not go to the heart of the matter.

The Federal Chancellor had to reply that these supposedly secondary and tertiary issues were in fact the most pressing ones. "What do the people get out of recognition?" is the headline over the speech by Federal Chancellor Brandt in the Bulletin of the Press and Information Office of the Federal government. This sentence does not actually appear in the Federal Chancellor's statements, but this is what those statements amount to. It was essential, Brandt maintained, that in the present serious situation a treaty between the two states should not only lay down broad objectives, but should present measures designed to deal with the problems peculiar to the two states alone. Stoph in his inflexible "all or nothing" approach did not make it clear "what positive results would emerge for the populations in the two German states from the existence of conditions of equality between the Federal Republic and the GDR."

Brandt's attitude can be summarised as follows: the GDR is only thinking in terms of the two states on German soil, not of the German nation. Once more Brandt outlined his conception of the nation:

> We see it in this way: the concept of the nation has its main roots in the past. "Nation" in our eyes means more than a common language and culture, but also more than a state and social order. It reposes on the sense of community among its people. And in this sense, there is in our opinion a unified nation. This unity is a thing which neither you nor we can do away with.

Brandt declared emphatically that the Oder-Neisse line and the Munich agreement could not be the object of negotiations between the Federal Republic and the GDR.

Nor could the existing treaty obligations be called into question. Until the establishment of a European peace system they formed the basis of European security. The two states could only negotiate within the context of the present treaties. "Because of their need for security the two German states have become allies of the victors in the east and west respectively. If we want to reinforce peace in Europe, we can only do so on this basis."

For this reason the Federal government was not in a position to agree that a precondition for regularising relations between the two Germanies would be willingness "to call into question the existing treaty systems and our involvement in them."

In this respect, the Kassel talks could go no further than to agree to disagree.

The Prime Minister of the GDR proposed a suspension of the talks to allow time for consideration.

In a debate in the Federal parliament which followed on the Kassel talks, the Federal Chancellor expounded his reasons for believing why they had been a success despite everything.

I should like to summarise the result of my two conversations so far with the Prime Minister of the GDR in this way: we know our two positions and both sides have thoroughly thought them out, and as a result the basis for the continuance of political conversations has taken on a more concrete form. That is my summary in brief. In order to achieve this—and this fact cannot be swept aside—Erfurt and Kassel have been absolutely essential from a political point of view.

The objective of the negotiations was "to reduce the confrontation by maintaining the balance."

Strauss, Kiesinger and von Guttenberg voiced the opposition attitudes; their arguments form part of the historical picture of the government's initiative in foreign affairs. Franz-Joseph Strauss took the view that the Federal Republic was reviving the old notion of "a vague concept of Germany."

The Federal government has chosen to use arguments based on a very superficial brand of pragmatism to erode their fundamental position in the German question, and are prepared to yield a great deal of ground in this respect, despite the fact that they have for twenty years been supported by all the democratic parties of this country.

These basic positions had, he continued, made the free part of Germany into an important factor in international politics in east and west and also in the third world. But now the unfortunate reputation of German vagueness weighed upon them again.

The Federal Chancellor, it was asserted, was not taking full account "of the true significance of the fact that in the last twenty years, after all the uncertainties and imponderables of German history, we have once again grown into a highly respected, reliable state which honours its treaty obligations," nor did he recognise "what damage a falsely understood flexibility and willingness to be accommodating in the face of the immediate realities of power must cause Germany's position in the world."

Former Chancellor Kiesinger put forward the old argument that Soviet policy had set itself the objective of dominating the whole of Europe, and continued to pursue this end; and apparently the Federal Chancellor felt he could no longer resist.

Freiherr von Guttenberg was the mouthpiece of a misguided idealism which an enthusiastic people had foolishly followed for twenty years. With high-flown and impressive passion—which harked back to the nineteenth-century movements towards freedom and nationalism—he attacked all forms of "injustice" and the use of force.

No one can relieve us, the freely elected representatives of the German people, of the obligation to concern ourselves with the fate of our entire nation.... We too know, and no one needs to tell us, that legal

> titles alone cannot form the basis of policies; but that they are essential instruments of a policy of freedom; for the law has always been the weapon of the weak and the peace-lover.
>
> Who would venture to say that the Germans over the frontier had already made their own private peace with foreign rule and suppression for as long as a foreign power prevented the people there from expressing unambiguously their political will. . . .
>
> We, the CDU and CSU, do not know either when the hour of freedom will sound for those on the other side of the wall and the barbed wire. But this we do know: that it will never come if we, the free German people, were ever prepared to bend the knee before brute force and naked power.

Again the issue was raised as to what concessions the Federal Republic had made by initiating negotiations on a basis of equality with the GDR and to what extent it had thereby given way to the two-state theory of Moscow. Again the discussions brought to light that the foundation of the Federal Republic and the GDR was the root cause of Germany's present divided condition.

To modify a phrase by Chancellor Erhard, a little bit of statehood is as plausible as a little bit of pregnancy. Adenauer, the founder of the Federal Republic, knew very well that one day the policy of refusing to acknowledge the new states in the east would have to come to an end; it was a policy which was pursued with the utmost resolution for as long as it had any practicality at all.

Brandt told the Federal parliament that he had gained the impression from Konrad Adenauer's papers that Adenauer had sought an understanding with Moscow with great earnestness and courage, and that mere stubbornness and the repetition of familiar demands would be regarded as a waste of time, and would bring no good to either the Federal Republic or the Soviet Union. He had sought to make the reconciliation with France into a model for reconciliation with the states of the Warsaw Pact, and above all with the Soviet Union. He was too much of a realist to content himself with an artificial game of ideological formulae, grandiose utterances and verbal expressions of helpless protest.

The Federal Chancellor described, on the occasion of the anniversary of the uprising in the GDR, how hopes of reunification through the medium of free elections gradually faded, and how the situation developed from that point until Erfurt and Kassel.

The painful recollection of 17 June 1953, he said, should still be kept alive. The demand for free elections in the GDR became so insistent that the régime itself was powerless to contain the popular movement. Free elections would have brought national unity:

> Among all of us—in the parties represented in this chamber—the hope remained supreme that the victorious powers would succeed despite

> everything in paving the way to a unified German state, and that free elections would be the key with which we—the Germans on both sides of the dividing line—would be able to open up the gateway to reunification.

But at once a feeling of helplessness had mingled itself with the enormous excitement generated by our fellow countrymen's violent protests. No one had wanted unity at any price, at the price of war. Peace, said Brandt, was more important than German unity.

> Looking back, we can see the line which became more and more rigidly fixed and which for all that was respected by both sides in the political power game: I mean the line which cuts through the heart of our country, the line which has split our continent in two. In the seventeen years of which I have been talking, this line has become ever more deeply scored into the ground, even where it is not drawn in reinforced concrete. And it was politically cemented together by the guarantees of two pact systems and the might of the two super-powers which backed them up . . . and changes in that line are now out of the question.

On the eve of the 17 June the Chancellor, recalling what happened at Kassel and Erfurt, at the same time referred to the historical lessons to be drawn from the 17 June. It was now a question of the possible, not of the desirable. Erfurt and Kassel marked a beginning. These meetings had, he said, forced both states "to regard each other in a different light." From now on, protests and speechifying alone would not be enough. There was now a "direct challenge to come to grips peacefully with the problems of a divided Germany." Questions of principle and of practice should be considered together.

The discussions between the Federal Republic and the GDR were overshadowed by the Federal Republic's soundings in Moscow, which were soon to develop into negotiations proper. All but a few of those involved were united in the conviction that the treaty between the USSR and the Federal Republic took precedence and should determine the pattern of future discussions. Negotiations in Moscow were led by Secretary of State Bahr between 12 and 22 May in three separate rounds of talks. Up until then Hellmut Allardt, the ambassador, had negotiated with the Soviet Commissar for Foreign Affairs. In the fourth and fifth rounds of talks the results of the discussions between Secretary of State Bahr and Falin, the Head of the third European section of the Soviet Ministry of Foreign Affairs, were formulated.

Whatever the significance of the results, the negotiations themselves were an important event, for they were the first to have taken place since the visit of Adenauer. For the first time since then a foreign policy decision of the first order was given into the hands of the Federal Republic. And it was no coincidence that Brandt kept referring back to Adenauer. For Adenauer had had the good fortune to be operating at a time when minds had not yet been fully made up and the newly emergent state structures had not yet become inflexibly fixed. Integration with the west may have presented itself to the Federal Republic, but the form which this was to take was still open; there was still room for genuine political activity.

Brandt too saw himself confronted with a similar historical moment. The negotiations with the Soviet Union might at times almost take the breath away. This explains why the government sought to lay down clear guidelines, objectives and a frame of reference for these negotiations. This was expressed in a statement by the Foreign Minister in the Federal parliament on 27 May and by a formal government resolution put forward by the government spokesman Ahlers.

In the statement by Foreign Minister Scheel it is first made clear in detail what kind of treaty there will not be:

> No treaty in which the German option, as I have called it already, to seek a way towards a European peace order in which the German people can regain their unity, is excluded or even rendered more difficult, nor any treaty in which the German people surrender their right to work towards national unity.
>
> This government has declared—and it stands by this declaration—that it considers reunification of the two states to be unattainable for the present. But nowhere has the government stated that it is prepared to give up even the possibility of reunification. On the contrary, I stress that our partners in the negotiations must recognise that we neither wish nor are we able to enter into any obligations or accept any conditions which are contrary to our convictions and indeed to our constitution, according to which the free will of the people must be the determining force for the future of any state.

On the other hand, he continued, the Federal government was operating on the basis of the current European realities, as must any peace policy which did not want to be an echo of the past. And among these realities was the Oder-Neisse line:

> In this context too, respect of frontiers is also one of the most fundamental principles. It is indeed also part of the European realities that the Federal government does not intend to break obligations at present in force, and can therefore act only in agreement with its allies wherever specific limits are set to its negotiating powers.

Scheel spelled out where the difficulties lay in the negotiations: namely, in the efforts on the part of the GDR to annexe West

Berlin. The GDR was seeking recognition by all the territories in Europe currently in existence—with the exception of West Berlin.

> When Herr Stoph says that West Berlin is not only surrounded by GDR territory, but is actually part of that territory, that is an attempt to annexe pure and simple, to claim land against all the principles of the law. I cannot emphasise too strongly that we shall resist any such attempts. And besides, it should not be forgotten that the incorporation of East Berlin into the territory of the GDR is in contravention of the agreements made after the end of the war.

The allies of the Federal Republic, he went on, took the Berlin problem very seriously indeed. They had entered into talks with the Soviet Union with the intention of finding a more stable solution than existed at present with regard to Berlin, where the responsibility of the Allies remained unaltered.

It had been made clear enough by the Federal government that the settlement of questions relating to Berlin and the intended treaties with the Soviet Union, Poland and the GDR should form a single political unity: "Only when all questions are settled to our satisfaction can they be politically effective."

The Federal Republic was taking a step in the dark—knowingly, because a crucial element of its treaty negotiations with the eastern bloc states, the future position af Berlin, remained an unknown factor. Up until now the Soviet government had not yet given the least indication of its intentions and ideas in relation to the Berlin question.

> I will not conceal the fact that it would facilitate our negotiations in other places if the Soviet Union for its part would give some kind of indication in respect of the Berlin talks making clear its readiness to find for Berlin a solution appropriate to the will of the people involved there.

The Allies and the Federal Republic have also not produced new ideas on a reshaping of the state of Berlin, the divided capital of a divided Germany. They have regarded seeking new treaties on Berlin as too dangerous, because the Soviet Union and the GDR would grasp the opportunity to call into question the right to existence of the western enclave of West Berlin in the middle of the Soviet sphere of interest. One western demand that is constantly being made is that the communications links with Berlin should not be subject to interruptions, that is, that the arbitrariness and annoyances should be removed, and this is something which it would not hurt the Soviet Union and the GDR to concede, because it would do nothing to alter the fact that western communications with Berlin in technical and practical terms are at the mercy of Soviet good offices. Another issue to be resolved in a settlement of the Berlin question is the ending of the prohibition on the West Berliners from visiting East Berlin.

## THE MOSCOW NEGOTIATIONS

A declaration by the Federal government dated 9 June states that certain unspecified "guarantees" for West Berlin (close ties with the Federal Republic and freedom of access) should be a prior condition for the implementation of the non-aggression pact. In the declaration the expectations and the basic principles surrounding the negotiations with the Soviet Union are enumerated:

1. Future relations between the Federal Republic and the Soviet Union are to be founded on renunciation of force or the threat of force in exactly the same way as has been the case between the Federal Republic and the three western powers. That also holds good for the inviolability of territorial integrity of all states and their frontiers.

Threat of force and force itself must also be excluded from differences of opinion or matters of dispute which continue to exist after the conclusion of a non-aggression pact.

2. The attitude of the Federal government towards the Berlin question remains unchanged. It is based on the premise that the four-power talks should lead to securing close links between the Federal Republic and West Berlin as well as unlimited access to West Berlin. Without such guarantees it will not be possible to implement a non-aggression pact.

3. The validity of existing treaties and agreements with third parties remains unaffected by the treaty which is to be concluded. And this includes the Treaty of Germany.

4. The right of the Germans to self-determination remains unaffected by the treaty which is to be concluded. The constitution, inclusive of its preamble, is not a subject for negotiation.

5. The Federal government takes as its starting-point the view that the treaties which it is seeking to make with the Soviet Union, Poland and other states of the Warsaw Pact, especially the settlement of relations with the GDR on the basis of the 20 points presented to it in Kassel, should lead to the establishment and development of normal relations, and regards this policy for better coexistence among the nations and the securing of peace in Europe as a unity.

6. The Federal government notes with satisfaction that this policy is fully endorsed and supported by the three western powers as well as the member states of the EEC and the Atlantic Alliance.

The Moscow negotiations, which took place mainly between Secretary of State Bahr and the People's Commissar for Foreign Affairs, were hard and long. Agreement or a measure of agreement was reached on individual points which almost brought about a shift in the differing views. The parties to the negotiation outlined those points which they believed might constitute a basis for final negotiations. They drew up proposals of their own which in their view would meet the approval of the other side. The piles of papers grew; some of them were published in the west German press, mainly in the opposition press. These "indiscretions" occurred in a somewhat haphazard and arbitrary manner and gave hardly any indication of the nature of the published documents, or of what stage of the negotiations they represented, and how much of what was published represented material on which agreement had been reached; things like this always seem more rigid and final when they emerge from the twilight zones of secret negotiation into the glare of day. They have about them the indeterminate quality of papers which form part of a negotiation but which have not found their way into official discussion at diplomatic level and lack any kind of identifying marks (description, filing number, addressee).

This is the case with the most famous of these papers which indiscreetly became public property, the "Bahr paper," which gave itself out as a treaty draft drawn up by Secretary of State Bahr. The paper is a crucial source, because it points to a settlement of all matters of dispute between the Federal Republic and the eastern bloc countries. Only two of its points were taken over into the final treaty (recognition of the Oder-Neisse line and the frontier between the Federal Republic and the GDR). There is no value in speculating whether it represents a success on the part of the Federal Republic that the other settlement clauses did not appear in the final non-aggression treaty. It is true that it falls in with the original approach of the Federal Republic, namely, that a declaration on non-aggression was a matter of principle which should not be cluttered up with the settlement of individual issues. But some parts of the Bahr paper do indicate a shift away from this extreme position. The demand for recognition of the GDR under international law and the declaration of the invalidity of the Munich agreement are both absent. If these two matters had been taken up, the Soviet Union would have laid itself open to the accusation of having sought to impose a specific settlement on the member states of the Warsaw Pact for their treaty with the Federal Republic. The agreement between Bahr and Gromyko concerned appropriate solutions to matters of dispute between the Federal Republic and the eastern bloc countries, and was a recommendation not to be ignored. Those involved knew how the Soviet Union wished certain questions to be resolved. It depended upon the situation of the individual states whether they felt themselves able to ignore the wishes of the Soviet Union. The Federal Republic was least able to do so, if it wanted to take its policy of détente with the east to a proper conclusion. Whether or not it was spelled out in the treaty itself, the Federal Republic knew full well that its treaty of non-aggression with the Soviet Union would only become fully effective if and when treaties with Poland, the GDR and Czechoslovakia came into being. Since the Moscow agreement as contained in the Bahr paper, the GDR and Czechoslovakia have known that the Soviet Union intended to place no pressure on the Federal Republic towards meeting the extreme demands of East Berlin and Prague. But on the other hand nor had the Soviet government been trying to force the two countries to refrain altogether from making such demands. The Soviet Union had left room for manoeuvre in the negotiations between the Federal Republic and the eastern bloc countries, and had in so doing determined that some considerable time would elapse before the entire treaty network in eastern Europe came into operation.

The "Bahr paper" is crucial to an understanding of recent developments in Europe; more than the treaty which was finally drawn up, it shows the interrelationships within the state systems of Europe after the conclusion of the negotiations on non-aggression and recognition.

Clause One of the Bahr paper might have sounded like one of the many friendship treaties of the past, were it not for the fact that "normalisation" and "the real situation as it exists" had taken on a special meaning in the course of the confrontations and negotiations.

> 1. The Federal Republic of Germany and the Union of Soviet Socialist Republics regard it as an important objective of their policies to maintain international peace and to achieve a reduction in tension. They declare their commitment towards further normalising the European situation on the basis of the real situation as it exists and the development of peaceful relations in this spirit between all European states.

The second Clause obligates the parties to the treaty to non-aggression in the sense of the UN Charter.

The third Clause concerns the inviolability and permanence of frontiers.

> 3. The Soviet Union and the Federal Republic of Germany both agree that peace in Europe can only be maintained if no one challenges the existing frontiers. They undertake to respect without reservation the territorial integrity of all states in Europe within their present frontiers. They declare that they have no territorial claims against anyone, nor will they make any such claims in the future. Now and for the future they regard the territorial boundaries of all the states in Europe as inviolable in the form they have on the day of the signing of this treaty, inclusive of the Oder-Neisse line which constitutes the western

frontier of Poland, and also of the frontier between the Federal Republic of Germany and the German Democratic Republic.

Political philologists and virtuosi of diplomatic hair-splitting have "raised the question whether a state is making territorial claims" if at a "peace conference" it expresses wishes in respect of the frontier which "in the peace treaty is to be confirmed." International law is no help here; and that is because it does not concern itself with unreal situations. And little is more unreal than a peace treaty decades after the end of a war, when the soldiers of that war have become old men, and only a handful of the commanders and statesmen involved in the war are still alive, after the states which waged war have ceased to exist and powers which were never involved in the war are supposed to sign peace treaties with one another.

The statement that only a peace treaty would be able to draw the frontier line between Germany and Poland is even more fantastical. But it is there in black and white in the Potsdam agreement which the Soviet Union and the GDR value as the most powerful reality in Europe.

According to this clause, all frontiers "including" the Oder-Neisse line and the frontier between the GDR and the Federal Republic are to be understood. The significance of the recognition of the frontier between the two German states remains unspecified. The Federal Republic takes the view that a frontier had been recognised which was not in dispute. Recognition of the state on the other side of that frontier, which is the conclusion the GDR draws from this situation, is an entirely separate issue.

The Federal Republic was in fact bound—by the terms of the Treaty of Germany—not to alter the boundaries between itself and the GDR, and this came at a time when the politicians of the Federal Republic would rather have shaken hands with a leper than with a representative of Walter Ulbricht's GDR.

Clause Four lays down that the previous treaties of the two states would not be touched by this agreement, and this refers in particular to the treaties of the Federal Republic with the western powers including the military alliances and also the alliances and treaties of the Soviet Union with the member states of the Warsaw Pact, without any of these being mentioned specifically.

In accordance with Clause Five the treaty of the Federal Republic with the USSR and its treaties yet to be concluded with the other "socialist countries," especially the GDR, Poland and Czechoslovakia, should form a "unified whole."

It was evident from the outset that the Soviet Union wanted to hold the controlling influence in the new treaty system, simply in order to consolidate its leadership within its empire. Thus the clauses that followed outlined the kind of treaties the Federal Republic was later to conclude with the GDR and Czechoslovakia.

Clause Six contains a clear obligation upon the Federal Republic to conclude with the GDR a treaty on lines clearly set down. Recognition of the GDR under international law is not imposed on the Federal Republic.

> 6. The government of the Federal Republic of Germany declares its readiness to conclude a treaty with the government of the German Democratic Republic which will have the same binding power between them as the other agreements which the Federal Republic of Germany and the German Democratic Republic conclude with other countries. In accordance with this, the Federal Republic will formulate its relationships with the German Democratic Republic on the basis of complete equality, non-discrimination, respect of the independence and self-sufficiency of each of the two states in matters relating to their internal competence within their respective boundaries. The government of the Federal Republic of Germany proceeds from the assumption that relations on the part of the German Democratic Republic and the Federal Republic of Germany towards other states should operate on the basis that neither of the two states can represent or act in the name of the other abroad.

Clause Seven provides that the Federal Republic of Germany and the German Democratic Republic should work towards UN membership.

In Clause Eight the Federal Republic undertakes to conclude with the Czechoslovakian Socialist Republic a treaty agreeable to both sides on the "invalidity" of the Munich agreement. No decision is taken as to whether the agreement was invalid from the outset or has since become invalidated.

In Clause Nine the two powers concluding the treaty undertake to develop further their mutual relations, particularly in the industrial and cultural fields.

The tenth and last Clause of the Bahr paper "welcomes" the plan of a conference on questions of putting European security and co-operation on to a firmer footing. This conference could easily represent a means whereby the Soviet Union might reshape the military systems in Europe to suit itself. The Federal Republic "welcomes" this European security conference which the Kremlin is anxious should take place. That does not make it happen; and even when it does happen, that does not mean that Russia will necessarily evolve a new security system. If a new system is agreed upon, then it still does not automatically uproot the existing defence systems and tear NATO apart.

On 7 August, after tough negotiations, a treaty on non-aggression was provisionally signed by Federal Foreign Minister Scheel and Gromyko, the People's Commissar for Foreign Affairs. On 12 August Federal Chancellor Brandt and Kosygin, the Russian Prime Minister, put their signatures to the treaty.

If the wording alone is considered, the treaty could be regarded as no more than a bare document, largely declamatory in character. The principles upon which it is based are those which have a general validity throughout Europe: the parties to the treaty undertake to honour all frontiers and to exercise force against no one. Future historians and international lawyers who have nothing but the treaty before them will find it difficult to make out where and in what manner the parties to the treaty are in any way affected by it. It protects frontiers which are not theirs; the non-aggression announced in the treaty has no concrete force; the two countries—which are not neighbours and have no common frontiers—have no immediate matters to settle between themselves; they are not capable of directly applying force against one another, let alone for the fact that in the case of the Federal Republic the mouse is not likely to roar against the bear.

For all that, the treaty has its concrete and historical significance; and seldom has so general a treaty had such a specific significance. It remains a document with an extraordinary depth of meaning: it can serve as a diplomatic map of Europe as it emerged from the Second World War and assumed its virtually definitive form. The following is the text of the treaty itself:

> The high contracting parties, anxious to contribute to strengthening peace and security in Europe and the world,
> Convinced that peaceful cooperation among states on the basis of the purposes and principles of the Charter of the United Nations complies with the ardent desire of nations and the general interests of international peace,
> Appreciating the fact that the agreed measures previously implemented by them, in particular the conclusion of the agreement of 13 September 1955 on the establishment of diplomatic relations, have created favourable conditions for new important steps designed to develop further and strengthen their mutual relations,
> Desiring to lend expression, in the form of a Treaty, to their determination to improve and extend cooperation between them, including economic relations as well as scientific, technical and cultural contacts, in the interests of both states,
> Have agreed as follows.
> ARTICLE 1: The Federal Republic of Germany and the Union of Soviet Socialist Republics consider it an important objective of their policies to maintain international peace and achieve détente.
> They affirm their endeavour to further the normalization of the situation in Europe and the development of peaceful relations among

all European states and in so doing proceed from the actual situation existing in this region.

ARTICLE 2: The Federal Republic of Germany and the Union of Soviet Socialist Republics shall in their mutual relations as well as in matters of ensuring European and international security be guided by the purposes and principles embodied in the Charter of the United Nations. Accordingly they shall settle their disputes exclusively by peaceful means and undertake to refrain from the threat or use of force, pursuant to Article 2 of the Charter of the United Nations, in any matters affecting security in Europe or international security, as well as in their mutual relations.

ARTICLE 3: In accordance with the foregoing purposes and principles the Federal Republic of Germany and Union of Soviet Socialist Republics share the realisation that peace can only be maintained in Europe if nobody disturbs the present frontiers. They declare that they have no territorial claims against anybody nor will assert such claims in the future.

They regard today and shall in future regard the frontiers of all Europe as inviolate such as they are on the date of signature of the present Treaty, including the Oder-Neisse line which forms the western frontier of the People's Republic of Poland and the frontier between the Federal Republic of Germany and the German Democratic Republic.

ARTICLE 4: The present Treaty between the Federal Republic of Germany and the Union of Soviet Socialist Republics shall not affect any bilateral or multilateral treaties or arrangements previously concluded by them.

ARTICLE 5: The present Treaty is subject to ratification and shall enter into force on the date of exchange of the instruments of ratification which shall take place in Moscow.

Done at Moscow on August 12, 1920 in two originals, each in the German and Russian languages, both texts being equally authentic.

For the Federal Republic of Germany ...

For the Union of Soviet Socialist Republics ...

Thus the two states have undertaken, in accordance with Article 2 of the UN Charter, to refrain from the use or threat of force. This is the only point at which the treaty contains anything like guidelines for conduct. The UN could decide whether force was applied and the action to be taken. But the UN, because of the right of veto, would be incapable of taking any effective measures against any force applied by the Soviet Union and its friends.

For a state born in the spirit of the revolutionary idea, it was a real admission indeed that peace could only be maintained if all frontiers remained inviolable. The great socialist revolutionaries—in particular Marx and Lassalle—were of the opinion that reverence for the territorial *status quo* was a repugnant reactionary principle and that the fixedness of state structures opposed to the principle of revolution. But now the Soviet Union was defending the present state of territorial possessions in Europe as brought about by the victory of the Soviet state. And the Soviet Union defends all possessors and all victors. All frontiers are sacred. Even Switzerland and Luxemburg could be beneficiaries under the Moscow treaty. The other European states enjoy directly the protection of Article Two of the UN Charter, into whose obligations the USSR and the Federal Republic have entered.

At the signing of the treaty the Federal Foreign Minister handed over a letter to the Soviet People's Commissar for Foreign Affairs, in which the German right to national unity is reserved.

> Dear Mr. Minister, In connexion with today's signature of the Treaty between the Federal Republic of Germany and the Union of Soviet Socialist Republics, the Government of the Federal Republic of Germany has the honour to state that this Treaty does not conflict with the political objective of the Federal Republic of Germany to work for a state of peace in Europe in which the German nation will recover its unity in free self-determination.
>
> Accept, Mr. Minister, the assurance of my highest consideration.

So it is not the direct right of the Federal Republic to reunification that is being reserved, but the right to establish the preconditions for reunification.

"Germany as a whole" does however appear in the note which the Federal Republic directed at the western powers.

> The Government of the Federal Republic of Germany has the honour, in connexion with the impending signature of a treaty between the Federal Republic of Germany and the Union of Soviet Socialist Republics, to report the following:
>
> The Federal Minister for Foreign Affairs has in connexion with the negotiations put forward the views of the Federal government with reference to the rights and responsibilities of the four powers in relation to Germany as a whole and Berlin.
>
> Since a settlement on the basis of a peace treaty has not been arrived at, both sides took the view that the intended treaty did not infringe upon the rights and responsibilities of the French Republic, the United Kingdom of Great Britain and Northern Ireland, the Union of Soviet Socialist Republics and the United States of America.
>
> The Federal Minister of Foreign Affairs has stated in this context:
>
> The question of the rights of the four powers are unrelated to the treaty which the Federal Republic of Germany and the Union of Soviet Socialist Republics intend to conclude, and is untouched by it.
>
> The Foreign Minister of the Union of Soviet Socialist Republics has declared in this context:
>
> The question of the rights of the four powers was not a subject of the negotiations with the Federal Republic of Germany. The Soviet Union set out with the view that this question should not be discussed.

On the occasion of the signing of the treaty all the documents to which the treaty refers were laid before the German people.

The statement by the Federal government dated 3 October 1954 runs as follows:

> The Federal Republic of Germany has declared its readiness to formulate its policies in accordance with the principles of the United Nations Charter and accepts the obligations contained under Article 2 of that Charter.
>
> After its entry to the North Atlantic Pact and the Treaty of Brussels the Federal Republic declares that it will refrain from any measure not in accordance with the strictly defensive nature of these two treaties. The Federal Republic especially obligates itself never to seek to bring about by violent means the reunification of Germany or changes in the present frontiers and further to resolve all questions of dispute that arise between the Federal Republic and other states with peaceful means.

The relevant clauses of the UN Charter are as follows:

> *Article 2.*
>
> The Organisation and its Members, in pursuit of the Purposes stated in Article 1, shall act in accordance with the following Principles.
>
> 1. The Organisation is based on the principle of sovereign equality of all its Members.
>
> 2. All Members, in order to ensure to all of them the rights and benefits resulting from membership, shall fulfil in good faith the obligations assumed by them in accordance with the present Charter.
>
> 3. All Members shall settle their international disputes by peaceful means in such a manner that international peace and security, and justice, are not endangered.
>
> 4. All Members shall refrain in their international relations from the threat or use of force against the territorial integrity or political independence of any state, or in any other manner inconsistent with the Purposes of the United Nations.
>
> 5. All Members shall give the United Nations every assistance in any action it takes in accordance with the present Charter, and shall refrain from giving assistance to any state against which the United Nations is taking preventive or enforcement action.
>
> 6. The Organisation shall ensure that states which are not Members of the United Nations act in accordance with these Principles so far as may be necessary for the maintenance of international peace and security.
>
> 7. Nothing contained in the present Charter shall authorise the United Nations to intervene in matters which are essentially within the domestic jurisdiction of any state or shall require the Members to submit such matters to settlement under the present Charter....
>
> *Article 53*
>
> 1. The Security Council shall, where appropriate, utilise such regional arrangements or agencies for enforcement action under its authority.

But no enforcement action shall be taken under regional arrangements or by regional agencies without the authorisation of the Security Council, with the exception of measures against any enemy state, as defined in paragraph 2 of this Article, provided for pursuant to Article 107 or in regional arrangements directed against renewal of aggressive policy on the part of any such state, until such time as the Organisation may, on request of the Governments concerned, be charged with the responsibility for preventing further aggression by such a state.
2. The term enemy state as used in paragraph 1 of this Article applies to any state which during the Second World War has been an enemy of any signatory of the present Charter.

*Article 107*

Nothing in the present Charter shall invalidate or preclude action, in relation to any state which during the Second World War has been an enemy of any signatory to the present Charter, taken or authorised as a result of that war by the Governments having responsibility for such action.

# THE ODER-NEISSE LINE

The treaty with Moscow is a turning point in the post-war history of Germany, and it would remain so, even had it not been ratified, because it is not the fairly sparse contents of the treaty that matter but the fact that a treaty was concluded at all. It derives its importance from the decision to create peaceful conditions in eastern Europe, from which it grew.

The undertaking by the Federal Republic to enter into negotiations with its "eastern neighbours" and to conclude a non-aggression pact with them forms the real core of the treaty between the Soviet Union and the Federal Republic.

Perhaps a new government might change the treaty, perhaps not even implement it, but it could never revoke what has become irrevocable nor take up arms against something which for the foreseeable future is unalterable. The German people can scarcely return again to a policy which would declare war on all the political systems and frontiers of eastern Europe.

The wording of the treaty would be foolish if the text itself had been of any great importance. "Non-aggression" has no real meaning either for the Federal Republic or the Soviet Union. In practical terms, the Federal Republic simply is not in a position to apply force against anyone. Besides, it is bound by several treaties not to pursue its ends by force.

Judgement as to whether the Soviet Union is exercising force, and the establishment of measures of any kind against Russian aggression can be blocked by the Russians themselves through the power of their veto. The Soviet Union can never be made a defendant, because it is itself always in the position of judge.

The positive content of the treaty lies principally in the obligation on the part of the Federal Republic to conclude additional non-aggression treaties with Poland, the GDR and Czechoslovakia. In this respect it is made explicitly clear that a mere declaration of good will and preparedness for peace in all three cases is not enough, that what was necessary instead was a concrete and direct implementation of a declaration of principle. The treaty lays down the principle that the most important and most fundamental means of putting the concept of non-aggression into effect would be solemn recognition of the inviolability of present frontiers. So in effect the Federal Republic was placed by the Moscow treaty under an obligation to conclude a frontier treaty with its three most important neighbouring states to the east, namely with Poland, the GDR and Czechoslovakia.

In the Moscow agreement the frontiers which the Federal Republic is to recognise are referred to by name: the Oder-Neisse line, and the frontier between the GDR and the Federal Republic. Both frontiers are unfortunate examples of a general principle. The frontier question is not the real point at issue in relations between the Federal Republic and the GDR. Recognition of the mutual frontier certainly protects each of the two states from attack by the other, but would do nothing positive about relations between these two different kinds of state which have grown up on the territory of the old Reich.

As far as Poland is concerned, the Polish government understandably protested against the subordination of the German-Polish frontier question to the broader frontier issues in Europe as a whole. The Oder-Neisse line was too hotly disputed in Polish history and bound up with too many human problems for Poland to accept that the Oder-Neisse line could be seen in the same terms as the frontier between Luxemburg and Germany. Thus it was evident that Poland would not look favourably on separating off the recognition of the Oder-Neisse line from the non-aggression issue. Recognition was the focal point of attention, and non-aggression was seen merely as a side-issue which would offer little more than corroboration of such recognition.

The Moscow treaty between the Soviet Union and the Federal Republic of Germany only lays down that negotiations between the Federal Republic, the GDR, Poland and Czechoslovakia should take place; what is not specified by the Soviet Union are the demands these three powers might make. There was no demand in the treaty for recognition of the GDR under international law, nor that the Federal Republic should declare that the Munich agreement was null and void from the outset.

It was evident that the Soviet Union did not wish to exert any pressure on the Federal Republic to conclude treaties with these three states on the basis of their demands. It could equally be assumed that the Soviet Union would exercise no pressure on these three countries to conclude a treaty with the Federal Republic only on the latter's terms.

The Oder-Neisse line seems inseparably bound up with the Potsdam conference. But it was actually established before in the conference in the Crimea, the Yalta conference, where the preconditions for a later settlement on the basis of peace treaties had yet to be laid down; so in a sense the groundwork for the Potsdam conference had been done there.

The Soviets had removed the territories east of the Oder-Neisse line out of the German zone of occupation and placed them under the "temporary administration" of Poland; the Poles and Russians were engaged in making a "clean sweep," that is, transferring the Germans from the territories east of the Oder-Neisse line and creating a purely Polish national state.

The Russians had already become involved in these territories which they had yielded up to Poland after the Soviet-Polish war of 1921.

The creation of the Oder-Neisse line was a compromise. Poland was to be compensated for its lost territories to the east which were not Polish occupied by German territory to be made Polish.

The western powers had to recognise in Potsdam that they were confronted with a fait accompli; and the coming years were to demonstrate that it was irreversible.

So the western powers in Potsdam gave their assent to these changes in Germany, but linked their approval to the condition that the definitive settlement of the Polish western frontier should be postponed until the peace conference. This it was that overshadowed the whole dispute about the recognition of the Oder-Neisse line and the readjustment of German-Polish relations. A peace conference would be left precious little room for manoeuvre when the transfer of the "German population or parts of the same remaining in Poland, Czechoslovakia and Hungary" agreed upon in Article 13 of the Potsdam conference was fully completed. The Soviet People's Commissar for Foreign Affairs at once expressed his doubts as to whether a frontier line could be regarded as temporary if any change in it would mean the re-transfer of millions of Germans back into their traditional territories.

Does this mean that fixing the frontier in Potsdam should be understood as a "delimitation," as an adaptation to local conditions of a frontier already broadly settled upon or as a complete redrawing of the frontier?

The text of the Potsdam agreement, which deals with the Polish frontier to the west, runs as follows:

> In conformity with the Agreement on Poland reached at the Crimea Conference the three Heads of Government have sought the opinion of the Polish Provisional Government of National Unity in regard to the accession of territory in the north and west which Poland should receive. The President of the National Council of Poland and members of the Polish Provisional Government of National Unity have been received at the Conference and have fully presented their views. The three Heads of Government reaffirm their opinion that the final delimitation of the western frontier of Poland should await the peace settlement.
>
> The three Heads of Government agree that, pending the final deter-

mination of Poland's western frontier, the former German territories east of a line running from the Baltic Sea immediately west of Swinemünde, and thence along the Oder River to the confluence of the western Neisse River and along the western Neisse to the Czechoslovak frontier, including that portion of East Prussia not placed under the administration of the Union of Soviet Socialist Republics in accordance with the understanding reached at this conference and including the area of the former Free City of Danzig, shall be under the administration of the Polish State and for such purposes should not be considered as part of the Soviet zone of occupation in Germany.

Article 12 of the Potsdam agreement, which provided for the transfer of Germans from the territories east of the Oder-Neisse line, is worded as follows:

> The Three Governments, having considered the question in all its aspects, recognise that the transfer to Germany of German populations, or elements thereof, remaining in Poland, Czechoslovakia and Hungary, will have to be undertaken. They agree that any transfers that take place should be effected in an orderly and humane manner.
>
> Since the influx of a large number of Germans into Germany would increase the burden already resting on the occupying authorities, they consider that the Control Council in Germany should, in the first instance, examine the problem, with special regard to the question of the equitable distribution of these Germans among the several zones of occupation. They are accordingly instructing their representatives on the Control Council to report to their Governments as soon as possible the extent to which such persons have already entered Germany from Poland, Czechoslovakia and Hungary, and to submit an estimate of the time and rate at which further transfers could be carried out having regard to the present situation in Germany.
>
> The Czechoslovak Government, the Polish Provisional Government and the Control Council in Hungary are at the same time being informed of the above and are being requested meanwhile to suspend further expulsions pending an examination by the Governments concerned of the report from their representatives on the Control Council.

When the GDR and Poland concluded the Görlitz agreement "on the sacred and unalterable peace settlement," the Oder-Neisse line, it was claimed on the west German side that such an agreement was passing over the rights of the German people as a whole who alone could enter into such a treaty, and in addition was infringing upon the Potsdam agreement, according to which the frontiers could only be definitively established by a peace conference. But this peace conference became more and more unlikely as the years went by.

None of the victorious powers has shown any serious intention in the years that followed to call a peace conference and to settle the big questions of Europe and Germany. The peace conference is also something of a vain hope because the war resulted in the complete destruction of Germany, and there is no German national state left to conclude a peace with. Success has not met any attempts to resurrect that Germany against which the war was waged and with which any peace would have to be concluded. There has never been a war between the Soviet Union and the Federal Republic, nor between the USSR, the USA and the Federal Republic, let alone with the GDR.

The treaty provisionally signed in Warsaw on 18 November and ratified by the heads of government on 7 December bases recognition of the Oder-Neisse line—a term which nowhere appears in the actual agreement—on the principle of the inviolability of frontiers and the integrity of states, for this was a basic condition for peace. Non-aggression understandably does not take pride of place, because Poland wanted to avoid the impression that the Federal Republic was only undertaking not to change the Oder-Neisse line by force. There follows a provocatively simple declaration. The parties to the treaty declare that the existing frontier, whose line was laid down in the Potsdam agreement, "forms the western state boundary of Poland." Evidently this is the settlement of a fact which virtually no one can deny. No account is taken of the Potsdam agreement as a whole; it does not serve as an historical, political or legal basis, or justification of the Warsaw agreement. Again it sounds like an indisputable fact that the line of the frontier between Germany and Poland was "laid down" in the Potsdam agreement (only the line, not the actual boundary itself). But the historical background to the Oder-Neisse line, and its confirmation by the "big three"—albeit with reservations—are more than just historical facts; the reference back to the line of the frontier to the Potsdam agreement relates the determination of the frontier to an historical turning point, precisely because the Potsdam agreement itself has been completely set aside and has been consulted only on the line of the frontier. The phrasing also states that the Potsdam conference only established the "line" of the frontier—on the basis of a decision that had already been taken. Potsdam itself marked a "delimitation," a drawing of the frontier in general terms to be specified in detail in the peace treaty, where the "final settlement" of the frontier was originally, according to the eastern view, to be set down.

The reference in the Potsdam agreement to the peace treaty has been dropped completely. The proviso of a peace settlement still had some meaning when it had not yet been settled whether Poland would succeed in occupying the newly-won territories. Churchill warned in Potsdam that the Polish goose should not be killed by over-feeding; west German public opinion considered that after the evacuation of the German population the territory would be an uninhabited waste, the "land of the wolves." At first no one saw further than the fact that millions of Germans had lost a home; only slowly did it become clear that at the same time millions of Poles had gained one.

Whether the proviso of a peace treaty is to be found in a declaration to the western Allies, that the Warsaw treaty does not and cannot infringe upon their rights and responsibilities, can perhaps be proven with virtuoso legalistic argumentation; that is of little practical significance. It is true that the logical outcome of the four-power responsibility for Germany would be a peace treaty through which the four powers can be relieved of their responsibilities. The reasons for which the four powers have not found a common view of this responsibility continue to exist. The three western powers have welcomed the Warsaw treaty in their answer to the statement by the Federal Republic that their rights and responsibilities are not affected nor can they be affected without expressing how far these rights and responsibilities have altered in a changed world.

Great Britain and France let it be known during the Warsaw negotiations that they were not interested in the proviso of a peace conference. But for the time being the obligation to bear common responsibility for Germany—taken to its conclusion—can only be regarded as a "peace" which restores Germany to itself.

The "non-aggression" element is taken word for word from the Moscow treaty without its being related to the frontier question.

The declaration that neither side has nor will seek to raise territorial claims against the other already exists in the Moscow treaty; any appeal by the Federal government to the Soviet Union or Poland to change the existing frontiers by agreement is excluded.

Whether it would be a "territorial claim" if the Federal Republic were to state in an international gathering that a frontier of revision was desirable, is a somewhat unreal question. The Federal Republic is strictly correct in asserting that there is no absolute finality in the bilateral declaration that the Oder-Neisse line forms the western frontier of Poland. Poland has not made a pact for all eternity, and in the confusion of treaties and declarations a "last resort" may be hidden somewhere.

The main body of the treaty text runs as follows:

> The Polish People's Republic and the Federal Republic of Germany:
> considering that more than twenty-five years have passed since the termination of World War Two of which Poland was the first victim and which brought grave sufferings upon the peoples of Europe,
> mindful that during that time in both countries a new generation has grown up which must be secured a peaceful future,

desirous of creating lasting bases for peaceful coexistence and development of normal and good relations between them,
aiming at consolidation of peace and security in Europe,
aware that the inviolability of the frontiers and respect for the territorial integrity and sovereignty of all states in Europe within their present frontiers are the basic condition of peace,
have agreed as follows:

ARTICLE 1

1. The Polish People's Republic and the Federal Republic of Germany unanimously affirm that the existing border line the course of which was established in Chapter Nine of the decisions of the Potsdam Conference of 2 August 1945 as from the Baltic Sea immediately west of Swinoujscie and thence along the Oder river to the confluence of the Lusatian Neisse river and along the Lusatian Neisse to the Czechoslovak frontier, constitutes the western state frontier of the Polish People's Republic.
2. They confirm the inviolability of their existing frontiers, now and in the future, and mutually pledge to respect unreservedly their territorial integrity.
3. They declare that they have no territorial claims against one another nor shall they advance such claims in the future.

ARTICLE 2

1. The Polish People's Republic and the Federal Republic of Germany shall be guided in their mutual relations as well as in matters concerning the safeguarding of European and world security by the purposes and principles set forth in the Charter of the United Nations.
2. Accordingly, in conformity with Articles 1 and 2 of the Charter of the United Nations they shall settle all their disputes exclusively by peaceful means and in questions of European and international security as well as in their mutual relations they shall refrain from the threat of force or the use of force.

ARTICLE 3

1. The Polish People's Republic and the Federal Republic of Germany shall undertake further steps aimed at full normalisation and all-round development of their mutual relations, the lasting basis of which shall be the present Treaty.
2. They agree that the expansion of their co-operation in the fields of economic, scientific, technological, cultural and other relations is in their common interest.

ARTICLE 4

The present Treaty does not affect bilateral or multilateral international agreements previously concluded by the parties or concerning them.

On 19 November 1970 the text of the provisionally signed treaty between the Federal Republic and the People's Republic of Poland was handed over to the ambassadors of the three western powers in Bonn in the form of three identically worded verbal notes.

The treaty between Poland and the Federal Republic is neither a success nor a triumph on the part of the Federal Republic, for it sets the seal on the historical defeat of Germany. It was not signed in order to make some gain. Treaties of this kind are signed only when it is inevitable.

The Federal government had taken the terrible but necessary decision to ring down the final curtain on decades of German history and the great work of colonisation which for a long time embodied the pride, greatness and tragedy of Prussia. It had the courage to set itself against the illusion held by part of the German people that the dead can be resurrected. The treaty is of epoch-making significance; cutting off the territories to the east of the Oder-Neisse was the most far-reaching event in German and Polish history for centuries, a shrinking of German territory such as had not taken place for more than five hundred years.

What could be offered in return for such a terrible decision? The old principles of give and take were not applicable. There is nothing that can be offered in return for a nation that breaks off a hopeless struggle, and the struggle was indeed hopeless. For no one was prepared to make the slightest move to help to restore the Germans to their territories east of the Oder-Neisse line.

For Britain the Oder-Neisse line was a means of stilling the voice of conscience which continued to nag after Britain's betrayal of Poland in 1939. France cannot have been aware of the fact that the unequal balance of population between Germany and France had now tipped in Germany's favour. In America the notion of the "cordon sanitaire" persisted, of buffer states between western Europe and the Soviet Union, in which Poland was to play a key role. And there were too many Poles living in the USA for the United States to take the side of Germany against Poland. But the might of the Soviet army was always on the alert to march in defence of the Oder-Neisse line.

The greatest upheaval in the history of the European nations, the transfer of ten million Germans and an influx of an equal number of Poles, was not negotiated, nor even touched upon.

But the Federal government wanted to make some gesture towards the Germans who had been so severely hit by these events. They did not fancy returning home with "empty" hands. But it would have been better if they had not forced the Poles into presenting the note on reuniting families, for it makes a mockery of a return gesture. The Polish statement is called "Information" and it does sound as if it had been put together by irritated officialdom. It reveals clearly that Poland does not want to get involved in the politics of minorities again and wishes to hear no more about "nationalities." It wants to keep the people it has already. The Polish statement disputes the figures given by the Federal Republic, which vary between several hundred thousand and a million, and states that at the very most a few tens of thousands might have been affected by measures directed towards bringing families together again.

The text runs:

> The government of the People's Republic of Poland has given the following information to the Federal government on measures towards the solution of humanitarian problems:
>
> 1. In 1955 the Polish government recommended the Polish Red Cross to come to an agreement with the Red Cross on reuniting families, as a result of which up to 1959 about a quarter of a million Poles have left the country. In the years between 1960 and 1969 about 150,000 further people left Poland through normal channels. In the matter of reuniting families the Polish government has always let itself be guided by humanitarian principles. It cannot agree that its positive attitude in the question of bringing families together was exploited in order to obtain persons of Polish nationality.
>
> 2. Up to the present a certain number of people of indisputedly German nationality and people of mixed family have for various reasons (for example, close connexions with place of birth) remained, and among them in the course of the years this feeling of belonging has come to dominate. The Polish government takes the view that persons who on the basis of their undisputed German nationality wish to emigrate to one of the two German states, can do so provided that this falls within the laws and legal provisions obtaining within Poland.
>
> In addition, the situation of mixed families and separated families as well as such cases of Polish citizens will be taken into consideration who, either as a result of changed family circumstances or as a result of changes in the decision they had taken at an earlier date, express the desire to be reunited with their relatives living in the GDR or the Federal Republic.
>
> 3. The competent Polish authorities have not had to deal with anything approaching the number of applications for permission to move to the Federal Republic that has been claimed in the Federal Republic. According to investigations to date by the Polish authorities, the criteria according to which emigration from Poland to the Federal Republic or the GDR can justifiably apply to a few tens of thousands of persons. The Polish government will therefore issue the appropriate instructions with a view to undertaking careful investigations as to whether the applications which have been handed in are justified and with a view to processing them in the shortest possible time.
>
> The Polish government will give the Polish Red Cross authority to accept lists of persons from the Federal Republic Red Cross whose

applications are in the hands of the German Red Cross in order to compare and carefully examine these lists with the corresponding compilations which are in the possession of the competent Polish authorities.

4. The collaboration between the Polish Red Cross and the Red Cross of the Federal Republic will be facilitated by all possible means. The Polish Red Cross will be given the authority to accept additional information on the lists from the German Red Cross and to inform it via the Polish authorities of the result of the examination of the applications which have been handed over. In addition, the Polish Red Cross will be further empowered to enter into joint discussions with the Federal Red Cross on all practical measures that might result from this action.

5. As far as the movement of persons is concerned, and particularly in relation to visits by members of the family, the competent Polish authorities will, after the treaty has come into force, apply the same principles on the basis of normalisation of relations between the two states which are usual in relation to other states of western Europe.

No German and no German state has ever lost anything in previously concluded treaties which was still possessed or which could hope to be regained. But in the case of Berlin and the relations between the two Germanies it is different. Here the Germans might lose what they still held. Here Germany and the Federal Republic are still fighting on; the fight will only be given up where it has become utterly hopeless.

It is not by chance that Federal Chancellor Brandt frequently refers back to Chancellor Adenauer. Adenauer himself has seen the results of his handiwork. If the very fabric of the Federal Republic was forgotten in the intoxicating slogans of reunification, the first impulse of this Republic was nevertheless to free itself from that other Germany, to fight passionately to prevent itself from being dragged down into the chaos and destruction of all Germany.

Herbert Wehner praised Adenauer for his work of reconstruction, for filling a vacuum with order and vigorous growth. But something was built up on the other side of the frontier too; it was only for a little while that the Federal Republic found itself next to a vacuum. There on the other side arose its likeness, another Germany, which obeyed the same laws of separate existence as the Federal Republic.

Even Adenauer knew that a future Germany could not be formed by obliterating the other Germany, that a new Germany, if it ever came, could only be constructed upon the foundations of the existing Germany. In the foreseeable future there can be no alternative but a Germany composed of two Germanies. Brandt's government is essentially doing no more than completing the journey which began with the formation of separate German states.

With remarkable consistency, the Federal Republic is advancing into the future in accordance with the constitution upon which it was founded. Only at the end of this path can there be a new beginning.

# POSTSCRIPT

This book, which I am now pleased to see appearing in English translation, was completed in December 1970. Since that time the treaties with Moscow and Warsaw have been broadened and supplemented by a four-power agreement on regularising traffic with Berlin and agreements between the senate of the city of Berlin and the GDR government. Not unexpectedly, none of these arrangements alters the basic situation in Europe. The Berlin settlements more or less normalise communications links between West Berlin and the Federal Republic. For the first time it has been recognised that *Germans* travel to Berlin, not just members of the occupation forces. Previous agreements on communications with Berlin had only related to the occupation forces. This Berlin agreement among the Allies recognises for the very first time, formally if in rather imprecise terms, that there is a relationship between the Federal Republic and West Berlin, although it is explicitly stated that West Berlin is not part of the Federal Republic. But it is down on paper in black and white that the Soviet Union and the GDR refrain from incorporating the whole city of Berlin into their territorial area. Things have stayed just as they were after the power struggle between the victorious allies in 1944-5: a divided Berlin, a "western Berlin," a separate city state, not subject to the GDR. Citizens of West Berlin may once more visit East Berlin in limited numbers and on receipt of official permission.

The culmination of Brandt's Ostpolitik came in May 1972, when the Bundestag ratified the treaties with Moscow and Warsaw. Earlier in the same month agreement had been reached on the Treaty on Transport Questions between the two parts of Germany.

The result in the German parliament was not achieved without considerable difficulty: as government and opposition were virtually in a state of numerical balance, Brandt sought an accommodation with opposition leader Dr. Rainer Barzel. The outcome was victory for Brandt, but a victory marred by local political wrangling. *The Times* first leader for 18 May 1972 states:

> The impact of the treaties has been reduced by their failure to win a broad majority and by the undignified haggling which has surrounded their passage through parliament. Only Herr Brandt and his party emerge with credit, having patiently tried to reach a compromise that in the end was not honoured.

So, although Brandt won this battle, his political future was far from secure. None the less, there is no doubt that May 1972 will be regarded as one of the most significant months in the entire post-war history, not just of Europe, but of the world at large: not only were treaties between Bonn and the east ratified; at a ceremony in Moscow, the seal was set on the new relationship betwen east and west when President Nixon and the Russian leaders signed the nuclear arms limitation treaty.

Right up until the elections which the parliamentary stalemate rendered inevitable, Brandt's political future hung in the balance, and with it the destiny of much of his Ostpolitik. But the November 1972 elections have returned his socialist and liberal coalition with a landslide majority which now seems once and for all to have swept aside the dark days of confrontation in the cold war and to pave the way towards even greater links with the east, as the signing of the treaty with the GDR demonstrates. The ultimate objective of a single united nation within the context of one German state may still seem remote, unattainable even, but the barriers between the two Germanies continue to come down. All that is needed is the maintenance of a positive and open spirit of co-operation; as the Federal President, Gustav Heinemann, expressed it on the occasion of the ratification of the treaties with the east in May, 1972:

> The debate was hard-fought.... But a past battle must not be fought on and allowed to prejudice the future.... What we must now do on both sides is to fill the treaties with life. If the nations do not make the treaties into a part of themselves, they will be nothing more than lifeless letters on the page. The confrontations of past years must now be translated into collaboration for the future.